the Padre puzzle

A MYSTERY NOVEL

DAVID HARRY

DEDICATION

Throughout my life the creative process, in all its manifestations, has fascinated me. For over forty years I have worked with some of the world's most creative scientific minds. Their foresight and technical accomplishments stand as a tribute to them and inspiration for us all. This book is dedicated to all the inventors I have had the privilege of working with all these years.

This book is also dedicated to Don Nichol of blessed memory.

DISCLAIMER

South Padre Island, the setting for *The Padre Puzzle*, is a crown jewel of the Texas Gulf coast. SPI, with miles of unbroken soft sandy beaches, dolphins playing in the surf, and warm delightful water, is a wonderful place to live, or just spend summer vacation.

I hesitate to set SPI at the center of an unfolding mystery, where dead bodies are found on the beach and drug lords smuggle narcotics, for fear of spoiling the image of a tranquil island in the sun.

But readers of mystery stories rise above thinking ill of a place where imaginary stories are set. I publish this work of pure fiction trusting the Town Fathers—and Mothers—will not speak ill of me, nor will they cut the utility services to my home.

The story told herein is a work of fiction and the characters, except for a few local South Padre Island individuals, as well as certain business establishments and landmarks, are purely fictional. Any dialog or thoughts pertaining to any actual person is a product of my imagination.

Printed in the United States and published by Hotray LLC

ISBN: 1453606793
ISBN-13: 9781453606797

ONE

My name is Jimmy Redstone. I'm a Texas Ranger, now on a temporary, some would say permanent, leave of absence. The leave came because, on my fifty-first birthday, I was shot in the left shoulder apprehending a bank robber who went by the trite handle of Badman Tex.

My version is that the perpetrator shot me, causing my gun to discharge with the bullet from my weapon passing through Tex's skull.

However, the ballistics experts, with the force of modern science solidly behind them, testified that my partner Lonnie Turner and I had two major facts wrong. First, the trajectory of the bullet that passed through my shoulder is consistent with it having come from the location inhabited, at the time, by Lonnie. Second, and this is what had, and in some circles still has, everyone skeptical, the experts believe that Badman Tex's gun was fired after he died.

Neither the bullet from Tex's gun, nor the bullet that was discharged from Lonnie's weapon, were recovered, leading to speculation that one or both of us disposed of the bullets.

Lonnie and I were both placed on administrative leave while the mess was sorted through. Tests for gunpowder, or any other sign that either of us pulled the trigger of Tex's gun, proved inconclusive.

Two years have passed since that time, and both Lonnie and I have now been cleared of any impropriety in what the Austin papers called *An Excessive Show Of Force*. The fact that the bank recovered over twelve million dollars with not one penny missing was not lost on the administrative judge. Nor was the fact that not one person stepped forward with a tear in his or her eye over the demise of Mister Tex.

I must admit, however, that I didn't help myself, when I got a load on one night and explained to all who would listen how the world was a much better place without the likes of Badman Tex. That bit of indiscretion found its way onto *YouTube* and then onto the front page of the paper. Even the networks ran that clip. The only thing I can say for myself is, "Good riddance, Badman! Every man, woman and child in Texas can sleep a little easier now that you've found your life's reward."

I've often since wondered if the papers would have thought my actions so excessive if it had been a load of their newspapers that Tex had stolen. Perhaps the more interesting question would be why anyone would bother stealing newspapers.

I was assigned a desk job, specifically, processing requests for search warrants and arguing their merits before various judges in Austin, San Antonio, or wherever the Rangers sent me. And it seems they took an uncommon delight in finding out-of-the-way courthouses for me to appear in. And let me tell you, Texas is one hell of a big place, covering over two hundred, sixty-two thousand square miles of land area with no seeming end to the number of off-the-beaten-path Court Houses. I feel as though I visited them all. If it hadn't been for my bum shoulder I would have been sent by horseback. That's how angry my tough-minded boss, Lieutenant Miller Contentus, was-and I believe still is-with me.

It also didn't help my cause when the papers published every nasty detail of the messy divorce I had been going through at the time of the shooting. That led to several contentious counseling sessions, followed by an anger-management seminar, followed by more counseling sessions.

I suggested to a counselor that it sounded to me like the proper police protocol was to carry water pistols, since this all started when I shot someone in the line of duty. That remark started the counseling cycle over again. The problem was, even though I had been exonerated, no one believed our story.

Lonnie is now back at his old job, but with a new partner. Some say he's on the watch list because he was assigned to a crusty old timer with a history of rehabilitating wayward Rangers. In Lonnie's case, this makes sense, because he's only thirty-two.

I'm a far different story. At fifty-three the consensus is that I won't change, and on-the-job rehabilitation will be nothing but a babysitting assignment that will end badly for all concerned. When I complained that I was being wasted, running all over Texas on admin duties, I was given a fitness-for-duty examination.

I failed because of the weakness in my shoulder and was promptly placed on leave. The official reason given for the leave is that I needed time to rehabilitate my shoulder. The good news is that my rehab bills are covered under the State Compensation Plan. The bad news is that, after six months of working on strength exercises, I am close, but not yet able, to do what I need to do, to get my fitness release.

Chasing bad guys is a lot more satisfying than chasing paper. And it's now clear to everyone that, if I go back to the last assignment I had chasing Court Houses, I'll eventually do something stupid and get canned. In the process, I might even lose my pension.

The phone rang. It was my boss. He had just received my updated fitness report and wanted me in his office first thing in the morning. Never a good sign. Lieutenant Contentus was not a morning person. For that matter I don't recall him being an afternoon person either.

The Texas Rangers building that housed our division was a discarded gray-block Court House on the edge of the business district, a block from Lady Bird Lake. The building was built with a minimum of windows, none of which were designed to open easily. It was as if the town fathers were afraid that with open windows the prisoners would escape. On reflection, maybe it was the lawyers they were worried about.

I was early for my eight o'clock meeting, learning long ago that with Contentus being on time meant you were late. It was his way of putting even hardened cops on the defensive. His office was small, probably in an earlier life it had been occupied by a Court Clerk. It held a desk, some filing drawers off to the side and two chairs. Its saving grace was a window behind the desk large enough for the full effect of the Texas State Capital building several blocks away to be felt by the Lieutenant's visitors.

"Nice of you to come by, Redstone. How's it going?" Contentus is not a big man, barely six feet tall, but his voice commands a room, any room, not just this closet of a space he calls home.

He knew full well how it was going. He also knew I had again not been certified. In fact, there was nothing the man didn't know. "You have the results," I answered, "you tell me."

"I'd say you're not ready to return to the field."

"That's what the doctor says. But he did say I was close. Within shooting distance of the goal." Poor choice of words, I know, but hey, you only go around once.

"Yes, I see that here." Contentus tapped the report for emphasis, making a pretense of studying the papers. From past dealings with him, I knew that was strictly for audience consumption. He knew what the papers contained, and he knew what he was about to say or do. The man was always in complete control. I waited quietly for his next move.

He studied me a moment, and then said, "Look, Redstone, you're a good man. Frankly, the reason you're still with us is that you're one of the best field men we have. The desk is not for you."

"So, are you saying it's over for me?"

"That's what I'm debating. I can't keep you on the desk. Not good for you. Not good for us. I can't put you in the field until you get your fitness cert."

"Seems that leaves me in no man's land."

"Look, you are close. I've made some calls. There's a guy down at South Padre runs a local gym. He's willing to take you in, run your ass off, get you in shape."

"Why the hell down there? There're gyms everywhere." Not that there was anything wrong with South Padre Island, a barrier island on the Gulf of Mexico, about as far south as one could go in the United States without traversing the border into Mexico. Some went so far as to call it the Texas Riviera. But if he was sending me away, I wanted to know the full story.

"You need to work your upper body. Rowing, kayaking, swimming, that sort of stuff. Being outside in the salt air might heal the muscles. Look, it might just be an old wives tale, but it can't hurt. You up for it?"

"I'm up for anything that gets my wings back. What can be bad with paid time at the beach?"

"Good." He pushed a card across his desk with the name of my lodging written on it. "Get your ass down there and get to work. I'll give you two months. Not a day longer. You're either certified or you're retired. That clear enough?"

"Understood," I replied, not knowing where this was going, but sensing Contentus was going out on a limb. "I'll be ready, the shoulder's almost there."

The salt water of the Gulf mixed with weight training and a program to strengthen my arm would either extend my career or kill it permanently. One way or the other, I was about to find out which it would be.

The *Island Fitness* gym where I was supposed to train was located on the second floor above a small strip mall toward the north end of the inhabited portion of the island. As I was about to find out, South Padre Island, or as it is affectionately known locally, SPI, attracts as diverse a population as one could find anywhere. At one time or another, a good percentage of the inhabitants find their way up the steps to the gym.

Mexican Nationals drive north from the border to vacation or live part-time on SPI, joining with Texans and others from as far away as Canada. Houston, Austin, and San Antonio are natural feeders, as well as Dallas, some five hundred and fifty miles to the north.

My observation has always been that such ends-of-the-earth places, of which SPI is but one example, attract a laid-back crowd who mostly desire having enough time in their lives to enjoy outdoor activities. SPI, with the beautiful blue-grey water of the Gulf of Mexico breaking gently along its endless miles of sandy beach on one side and the relatively shallow Laguna Madre Bay on the other, has just about any water-related activity a person could want.

Parasailing seems to be a popular activity and every time I cross the two and a half mile bridge from Port Isabel I vow to myself to take a ride. So far, I've not indulged myself.

Other than the owner of the *Island Fitness* gym, I know only one other person on the island. Lieutenant Mark Cruses is the thirty-five-year-old son of my first partner. Mark, who was baptized Markus Joseph Cruses, II, is now a career Coast Guarder and the resident senior officer at the Coast Guard station located at the south end of the island.

In a happier time, our families had often gone sailing on Austin's Lake Travis. That was when I was still married and before my son Lester decided I wasn't such a good father after all and headed up north to gain his freedom. He's now somewhere in Alaska, and the only time I hear from him is when there is some sort of emergency condition, usually involving money flowing in his direction. Lester is a year younger than Mark, chronologically, but light years younger in maturity. The two are not in the same league.

You could see it even when they were young boys. Mark would plan our trips long before we left the house and, as soon as we were on the dock, he would systematically get the boat ready. The lines would be properly checked and laid out, the sail cover taken off and stowed, the docking lines reduced to just the last two. He would do a radio check and make sure the flares were dry, all this while Les was busy with God knows what.

My partner, watching his son scurry around the boat, would roll his eyes and say, "What the hell we need flares for on Lake Travis? We can shout if we're in trouble! The boy read an article in some boating magazine, I think it was *Cruising World*, on preparedness for sea and he insisted we equip the boat for any contingency. I put my foot down when he wanted a spare starter. We compromised on a set of oars. I was afraid he was about to lobby for an extra mast."

"Better safe than sorry," I responded, to my partner's eye roll. "Not a bad trait in the lad."

"I suppose," Mark, Sr., said, "but he's trying at times. If I lay a tool out of place in the garage, the boy's all over me. I got him his own tools and told him to leave me alone. Trouble is, I need to borrow his set 'cause I can't find what I want of my own. So now he cleans up my tools every chance he gets."

"Les wouldn't know one end of a hammer from the other. Never been around anyone who works so hard to do so little."

"Must drive you nuts, Jimmy. You can't sit still, always looking to be sure nothing's left to chance. He's just the opposite. Ever think of sending him to one of those boot-type camps, straighten him out?"

"His mother won't hear of it. Says I've gotta stop picking on the poor baby. Says it's my fault he's the way he is! That's the new thinking, you know. Anything wrong with the kid, it's the Dad's fault. Hell, I tried to pull what he pulls, my old man woulda whooped my butt. He whooped my butt even when I did what I was supposed to do. If he caught me sitting around doing nothing, I'd get more to do than I could ever get done. No wonder I'm the way I am today. Old man would have it no other way."

I was thinking of my early conversations with old Markus, as I sat waiting for his son at the *Wanna Wanna*, an outdoor burger and beer place extending over the sand dunes less than fifty yards from the rolling surf of the Gulf. The fried shrimp basket was reported to be the best in town. There was nothing wrong with the live music either, nor with the parade of bikini-clad women passing back and forth between the adjacent motel and the beach. From what I could tell, this place attracted people from sunup to long after sundown, many sitting around the half circular bar that hung out over the sand. A thatched roof coved the bar area, protecting the regulars from sun poisoning. They were on their own to protect themselves from the rigors of alcohol.

I'm beginning to understand the pace of life on this delightful spit of land and happy that I've settled in for the rehab work. Teran, the owner of the Sweat Shop, the name I gave to his gym, mapped out a rigorous set of sessions with two-a-days on Tuesday and Thursday and a two-hour morning workout every other day except for Sunday. The afternoons he expected me to kayak, either on the relatively flat bay or in the rolling surf of the Gulf. "Start off with two hours a day," he commanded, "but I really want you up to four or even six. We'll get your shoulder back in six weeks time."

Teran's a good guy when he's not beating me up. I expected to see a guy with bulging muscles and a bad attitude toward those of us who are not in top shape, but I was wrong. He's a bit on the wiry side and tells stories with a pleasant smile. I've tried to explain to him I'm not concerned with my legs, just with my left shoulder. His response has been consistent, "It's all one system. Everything's connected. Got to strengthen it all together." Then, as if to rub it in, he added, "You're the guy who let yourself go. I only have two months to undo all your bad habits. Cut me a break and get with the program."

TWO

Tomorrow, after a week of building up my shoulder strength using all manner of machines and weights, I begin kayaking on the bay. Teran assures me it's gorgeous out there and good for my spirit as well as my shoulder. What the hell a trainer knows about spirits I didn't begin to ask.

Thinking of spirits, while I waited for Mark, who was normally punctual to a fault, I made my way under the thatching to the bar to get a Budweiser refill. The musicians had taken a break and several bathing suit clad men and a few women materialized in line ahead of me, all filling orders for some form of alcoholic beverage. The skin from the neck on down of the guy in front of me was bright red and I fought the urge to tell him to apply more sun block. I only hoped for his sake that he knew how to sleep on his tummy.

I was carrying the beer back to the table when I spotted Mark walking purposefully across the parking lot, his step as brisk as I remembered. When he spotted me, he sent a half salute my way. He was coming from work and was dressed in Coast Guard dark blue with the blouse outside his pants. Neat as ever. Looked like the man pressed his work clothes. He seemed to have grown since I last saw him and was abut an inch taller than I. That placed him at six feet one inch. His face had filed out and his formerly dark brown hair had turned auburn, most likely, from the sun.

"Nice to see you, Mr. Redstone. I'm glad you decided on the Island for your rehab. Teran will get you back on the job if anyone can."

"Mark, you haven't changed one bit! Please call me Jimmy. How many times have I told you that? How are you?"

"Yes, Sir. Pop told me to call you Uncle Jimmy. Is that okay with you?"

"That's fine with me." In fact, anything he called me would have been fine with me. He was more of a son than the one I barely knew. "Your mother getting along okay?"

"Losing Pop was a blow to her. She knew about the cancer but never thought it would take him."

"He certainly was a rock—to all of us," I replied. I actually missed him more than I let on.

"She's managing. I want her to come here for a while, but she's not ready. When I get some leave next month, I plan to bring her to the Island. She'll love the dolphins."

"I've heard about them, but haven't found the time to get out and see any, yet. I also promised I'd take myself parasailing, but haven't done that yet either."

"You should do the dolphins, they're worth the time. I hear you'll be kayaking. You could even get over there by kayak. They hang out by the station."

"How about you take me out when you have some spare time? I'd love for you to show me around. I understand it can be pretty shallow out there."

"In places, yes. Love to, but that might not be for a while. Hey, don't worry about the depth, kayak can go anywhere."

"You're busy then? You hungry? " I glanced over to the bar where the food orders were taken and saw that only one person, a gangly teen, was there, his elbows on the bar, his head bobbing to music only he could hear. "What do you want? I'll get it for you." He wanted a burger, passed on the beer, and asked for a Dr Pepper. I placed the order and came back to the table. We were sitting on a wide deck several steps below the covered bar. A canvas covering was strung overhead giving some protection from the bright sun.

The entertainment, locals, consisting of a keyboarder, a base player and a drummer, was still on break so it was easier to talk. When I sat down, Mark said, "Yea, we've been busy lately. Homeland Security got us running. But that's nothing new. Our job is patrolling the water border between Mexico and the US. You'd be surprised at how much uninhabited coast there is between here and the next town north."

"Judging from the number of T-shirt shops I wouldn't think there'd be an inch of space for anything."

"Not so. SPI, I mean the City, only goes about five miles north. Then there are some beach areas controlled by the county and then nothing until the channel cuts the island off from the northern part. Most of the island is barren. Put that together with the eighty or so uninhabited miles on the south end of Padre Island, that's the next island north, and we got a lot of area to patrol. It's ripe for mischief if we so much as turn our backs to catch our breath."

"You patrol all that by boat?"

"Oh, goodness no. Planes, and even helicopters, are on constant patrol. I'm only responsible for the water-based craft from the south. At the station, we can track everything that moves. You can come by and see the operation. You sit here, it seems that nothing is happening. You look at our monitors and you realize the water out there is a busy place."

"I'd love to come by. I'm surprised you can allow a non-military person to observe."

"You're not exactly an enemy of the country. I mean, being with the Rangers and all."

"On leave."

"That's 'cause of the arm, I mean shoulder. How's that coming along?"

"How did you know about the rehab? Not many people outside the Division were aware of what I was doing down here."

"Small place. Actually, I work out with Teran. And sometimes Patricia May joins me." A funny look crossed his face, as if he had just allowed a secret to slip out.

"And who may I ask is Patricia May?"

"My girl friend. Actually, as of two days ago, my financé." He blushed, "Now that's still private. We haven't yet told Mom."

"Any reason? I mean for not announcing the engagement. And more important, why haven't you told your mother?"

"Want to do it in person. Next weekend we're planning on driving to Austin."

"Has she met Patricia May yet?"

He reddened even more and his eyes momentarily glanced down. "Fraid not."

"Okay, what's up?" I studied Mark as he worked through what he was going to say—and not say. Mark was a good kid and a boy I would be proud to call my own. He had never been one to do anything that would displease his parents. I couldn't imagine what was troubling him.

"Trich, that's what she prefers to be called, is from Mexico. They're called Nationals." He hesitated, perhaps expecting me to understand. I remained passive. This was his story and he had to tell it his way.

"Pop, before he died, told me how proud he was to have overcome the heritage from his grandfather who came across the Rio Grande to pick cotton in Texas."

"Your father had nothing against Mexicans. We worked with several in the Rangers, and he had many friends who were from Mexico or of Mexican heritage. I never once heard him say anything negative. In fact, he seemed proud of his heritage."

Mark's forehead crinkled into a frown. He hesitated for a moment, and then replied, "That may be, but I have the distinct impression he would have been unhappy to see me marry a Mexican girl. He often spoke of how he had overcome the stigma of being the grandson of a National." He looked away again, embarrassed, but seemed resolved to get it on the table, to hear what I would say. "She's a wonderful person. We go to Church together, at least when I can get away from the station." He looked up, a sudden flash of the old Mark now visible. "Hey, how about joining us tomorrow? Our Lady Star Of The Sea, in Port Isabel at ten. Church is named in honor of the local fishermen. Once this was the largest shrimp fleet in the US. On hard times now, they barely eke out a living."

He was now studying me, hoping for a clue to what I was thinking. More precisely, he was desperate to know what impact Trich would have on his mother.

"I would be delighted to attend," I answered. "Got to confess, it's been awhile since I last went. I would love to meet Trich. You sure I wouldn't be interfering."

"Absolutely not. She's dying to meet you." His blushing deep-
ened. "Actually, we talked about this and decided it would be easier
if she met you before she met Mom. You'll like her."

"What does she do?"

"She's a nurse in Brownsville. I met her at the hospital when
a buddy got injured. We got to talking, and I ran into her at the
Church. It's gone from there."

"She live in Brownsville?"

"Matamoros. Walks across the bridge to work at the hospital."

We agreed on a time, and then I said, "You think marrying a
Mexican woman is dishonoring your father. Is that what's troubling you?"

Mark sat upright in his chair and took a long drink of soda. He
ran a napkin across his lips, as if to finish that phase of his activity
before beginning the next. "Pop and you were close, and you knew
how proud he was of what he had accomplished, the grandson of an
itinerate cotton picker. An illegal immigrant at that. I don't want to
disgrace him or his memory."

"He was proud of you in every way. The fact that you've grown
up with an open mind and without prejudice is a tribute to his
memory, not a dishonor. He never once said or did anything deroga-
tory to non-Americans of any nationality. Yes, he was proud of being
American—fiercely proud, I might add—but that doesn't foreclose
accepting other nationalities into your life."

"Will Mom feel that way, or are you just soothing me? Give it
to me straight, this has tore me up."

"I can't imagine your mother having any feeling other than what
I just said."

"I'm all she has now," he said, tenderness replacing concern.
"Since Pop died, she's been lost. She has her friends, but they did so
much together it's hard on her."

"How long were they married? It was about fifty years, if I recall."

"Over fifty years. Pop died at seventy-five, they were married when he was twenty-one, she was seventeen."

"That's a long time. I can understand why it's so hard for her. It's been over a year now. Is it getting any easier for her?"

"Maybe a bit. I don't get up there as much these last few months as I did at first."

"Spending time with Trich."

"That. But work also. Leave's been cut. We're just busy."

"Have things changed? What's going on?"

"Lot's of stuff, but lately there's a lot of activity with vessels of unknown origin entering our waters. We spot them usually by plane or satellite and track them. If they don't turn back or head off to Mexico, we dispatch and intercept them. They usually turn at that point. Our station monitors that activity. We don't actually get excited until they continue into our water."

"What's the issue? I mean, what are you concerned about?"

"Any number of things. Drugs primarily. That was our only real concern until this Homeland Security stuff got big. Now the brass's concerned about introducing weapons and terrorists. The uninhabited coast makes a great target for that sort of activity."

"Surely the local law enforcement won't allow people to just come ashore and wander around."

"They're great. Do a fabulous job, but that's easier to say than to do. With so much open space, it's hard to stop people from slipping off a vessel and paddling ashore at night. Believe it or not, there are individuals who make a living at slipping people and drugs ashore. And they're good at it."

"Can't you track the boats and know where they'd be?"

"Pretty much, but not perfectly. They slip in and out of the fishing fleet, often launching a small fast boat that makes a run for the

shore. It's hard to tell if they throw drugs over when they're in the
surf. They have campers staked out to retrieve the sealed packages,
that sort of thing. It's cat and mouse. Keeps us on our toes."

"Any thought the locals are in league with the bad guys?"

"That's above my pay grade," Mark answered quickly, as though
he had known I was going to ask. "I patrol the water for the Government. What happens on shore is not my mission."

"But you have your suspicions?"

"Not really suspicions. Just thoughts. The drugs are getting in
somehow, somewhere. That's a fact. Exactly how and where, that's
conjecture."

"You guys bust folks?"

"All the time. We seized nearly five hundred pounds of cocaine
about a month ago, just off the entrance channel." He pointed down
the beach. "That one came on a tip, I think from a plant we have
inside the operation. I have no idea of how much we didn't catch.
It's big business and sophisticated. They're smart enough to tip us to
a mule and, while we're busting the runner, they bring a bigger pay-
load ashore up the coast. We're busy slapping our backs, getting our
PR and they're hard at work delivering the real goods unmolested.
Our side issues press releases; their side delivers the merchandise."

"Look, if it makes you feel any better, we have the same problem. Before I was shot, I participated in several task forces in the
Valley. We got over two thousand pounds of drugs in one week. I'm
sure the day we went home, another two thousand pounds slipped
right in. In fact, like you said, while we were holding the bags up for
the photo op, they were busy delivering twice that amount a mile
away. I don't know if the locals are involved, but I do know there's a
bad egg every now and again. Money does tend to corrupt, but for
the most part, the locals do a great job."

"Pop sometimes talked to me about corruption and the investigations he was involved in. You do any of that?"

Now it was my turn to sidestep the topic. "As I said, there's a bad egg every now and again. The Rangers are called upon to investigate. Makes us a bit unpopular at times is all I can say."

THREE

The church in Port Isabel is tucked away in a neat neighborhood of modest homes not far from the waterway where the shrimp fleet made its home. Mark, as was expected, was on time, but without Trich. Before I could ask about her, he said, "She was called to the hospital an hour ago. A fire in an apartment building killed three people and one six-year-old was burned severely. They're trying to save his life. Trich is needed to coordinate. She sends her pardons."

"I understand. Work comes first."

"Speaking of business, I was paged a few minutes ago, got to go on in. Sorry to back out on you like this, you coming across the bridge and all."

"Hey, it's not like I had anything else going for me this morning. I'm sure I'll get to meet Trich in due course."

"Maybe tonight. I'll call when this operation is finished." He took a few steps toward his car and then turned back toward me.

I was trying to decide whether to continue on to church without him, when his voice cut through my deliberation. "How would you like to come out to the station with me? Meet some of the guys."

"Lead the way," I said, without hesitation.

In retrospect, I often wonder what would have become of my career if I had simply gone to church that Sunday morning. But the fact is, life is what happens to you along the way, so any amount of musing on alternate paths is essentially worthless.

The Coast Guard Station on South Padre Island is located south of the bridge connection, officially called the Queen Isabella Causeway, on the bay side of the island. I followed Mark to a small parking area beside the Station. Two sleek Coast Guard boats were tied up to protected docks behind a huge workboat with cranes and other nautical-looking devices that I wouldn't even venture to name.

Mark walked briskly across the parking area and assumed his command demeanor. All traces of doubt were gone from his face, as well as from his body. He was on duty and ready for anything thrown his way.

I was a few steps behind him and paused to glance around. At the far side of the parking area, a helicopter was tied down in a small clearing. Beyond the helicopter, several men were wading in the shallow water, fishing rods in their hands and nets hanging from their waists.

When I entered the station, Mark was already busy gathering information from several sources, seemingly at the same time. He was in a room with what looked to have over a hundred monitors all displaying different information. That room was separated from the main area where I was by a glass partition. He motioned to a uniformed young man who didn't look old enough to shave.

The man nodded and came back toward where I was standing. I expected him to say something to me, but instead he kept walking and, next, I saw him climbing down onto the smaller of the two boats tied out back.

A few minutes later, the boat backed away from the dock and roared to life into the bay, heading south toward the channel leading out to the Gulf.

Mark motioned for me to join him in the display room. When I did he said, "You can disregard the monitors on that side of the room," he said, waving his arm toward the left. "They simply give us wind and water temperature at various points, along with wave conditions and other environmental data that is useful but not critical. The important ones are these over here," he said, pointing to a wall of monitors on his right. "They show surveillance videos of different sectors. See the numbers on the bottom of each? They refer to the sector. There are also lat and lon numbers for precise pinpointing should we need to intercept."

"And what are those?" I asked, nodding toward several monitors where only words streamed across the screens.

"That's a visual readout of radio traffic. If we display the actual transmissions, we can monitor as many as we want at the same time. Right now, I'm watching six interactions. See the one in red? That's an emergency. Captain called in an SOS and that's where that vessel, the one that just left, is going. We've switched to channel twenty-two and cleared the channel."

"Who's handling the radio?"

"Got no one now. The guy I just dispatched was acting as our radioman. He's a new guy, just assigned here. Speaks Spanish fluently, and that's a plus down here."

"What's the nature of the emergency?"

"Taking on water faster than the pumps will empty the craft. It's a small private fishing boat with six people on board. I don't usually like to send a single guy out, in fact not supposed to, but I can't sit by and do nothing. It'll take about an hour before we reach them. Unfortunately, there's nothing we can do sooner."

"What if the boat sinks by then?"

"They've been instructed to all wear life jackets."

"Wasn't that a rather small boat to be going out into the Gulf?"

"Not on a day such as we have out there today," Mark replied, now the teacher. "After he makes it through the breakwater and gets a mile or so off shore, the water'll be relatively flat. Not always that way, but today it'll be fine. No weather coming in. We're lucky that way; weather doesn't surprise us. That's why I can send him alone. Small boat, no real weather to contend with."

"Another monitor went red. What's going on there?"

Mark studied the monitor for a while and then said, "This is a problem. Could be major; we'll know in a few moments." He returned his attention to the monitor and I tried to read along, but it didn't make sense to me.

Mark reached for the microphone, "Corpus, I'm going out, Station Padre will be unmanned until further notice."

Mark returned his concentration to the red monitor and, after a few minutes said to me, "Come, I'm pressing you into service. This is actually right up your alley. A shrimp boat captain is reporting at least one and maybe two bodies caught in their net."

"What do you want with me? I'm on leave."

"I can't go alone. The only craft I have requires help and it's going to take at least an hour before we can get someone else here. You're it."

"Not in these clothes. Wrong shoes."

"Got everything you need. We'll both change. I'll even get you an official Guard hat."

"What's the hurry? From my experience, dead bodies don't get any deader."

"Possibility one or both may be alive," Mark replied. "Corpus would dispatch a helicopter, but the one they usually use is being repaired and the other is already on patrol and is low on fuel. If we can get on scene sooner, then we will. We'll monitor the situation while under way."

In less than ten minutes, we were away from the dock and heading into the Gulf. Not surprising, Mark was expert at what he was doing. His orders to me for releasing the lines were just as I remembered from years earlier, crisp and concise. His seamanship technique had been honed to a fine edge over the years, and I settled back as a passenger, while the cutter moved smoothly through the water.

Mark was right; the water in the Gulf was relatively smooth, and except for the slow-rising swells I would have thought we were on Lake Travis.

Mark had set a waypoint on the SatNav at 26.145N and 96.803W, which meant nothing to me, but I noted our northeast heading of forty-five degrees. He told me we were going approximately twenty-five miles offshore.

I had nothing to do until we got there, but Mark, being Mark, wanted to make sure that I could operate the boat if he had to board the fishing boat for any reason, or otherwise became incapacitated. He showed me the controls, explained their operation, and then had me take over operation of the vessel.

When he was satisfied that I was comfortable at the helm, he instructed me to slow down and then stop. He had me put the boat in reverse and showed me how to maneuver in tight spaces with the

engines only, one in forward, one in reverse. By the time he was finished with his lessons I was ready to take the master mariner's exam.

When we got under way again, he even had me use the radio
and change frequencies. He instructed me on how to use the secure
channels. "We had to install the secure system 'cause the bad guys
were tracking our every move. They still do so, but it's harder now.
They have to be more sophisticated. But truth is, every move we
make, they make a counter move. Drugs are big business, and they
have a lot of money to throw around."

"How the hell do I get back if you fall overboard?" I wanted to
show him I was taking my responsibilities seriously. "It's too far to
swim," I added, "but truth is, Teran would applaud if I attempted
to swim from here."

"I'd hope you'd pick me up like we practiced when I was a kid.
Remember all the times we practiced man overboard drills?"

"I certainly do." I didn't want to add that we did those drills at
his insistence. "But what if I screw up and run over you?"

I was joking, but Mark was dead serious. "Watch what you're
doing and you won't run me over." Continuing with the lesson, he
said, "There's already a waypoint programmed into the SatNav for
the channel entrance. It's called BRNS ENT and here's how you set
it." He made me watch as he tapped a few buttons. "Just like the nav
in your car, if you have navigation that is."

Before I could answer, a message appeared on the screen. *Set
now?*

He checked *no* in the box.

"If you were going back now you would have checked *yes* and
then you would have been asked if you want self-steer. That's your
choice, you want to hand steer, you can do so, or if you want the
electronics to take you home, you can do it that way. Also, this
switch here…" he pointed to one of a dozen controls, "will allow

you to go back and forth between hand-steering and electronics. Just be sure you have the right waypoint programmed, or you'll find yourself a long way from home in a hurry. The good news is that by setting BRNS ENT the vessel will steer you home." In the same serious instructor tone, he continued, "Just be sure there's nothing between you and the waypoint, I mean by way of shallow water. Vessel draws six feet."

"That's not very deep," I said, trying to sound as if I knew what I was doing.

"The bay is shallow, so we need to keep the vessel's draft shallow." He was about to continue when the radio broke over.

"Corpus to UTB 303, switch and answer on secure 1."

"Acknowledge." Mark quickly dialed in the designated channel and remained quiet.

"Corpus to UTB 303," came the same voice, now on the secure channel.

"UTB 303 to Corpus. Go ahead, UTB 303 here," Mark responded, his body alert for every nuance of the transmission.

"Skipper," came an authoritative voice, "Your ETA."

Mark glanced at several readouts before responding, "Fourteen fifteen, Sir. Seven miles ahead."

"Visual?"

"Radar only. Haze limits visibility."

"Let me know immediately when you have visual. Remain on secure channel 1. Target is expecting a helo overhead. I want to know what they'll do when they see you coming. Helo2 is being held pending your instruction."

"Acknowledged."

"Out."

"Something's up," Mark said, when the radio snapped off. "That was Captain Boyle. He's three levels up from me. One tough guy.

Never heard him on the radio before. He leaves that to his field commanders, like myself. He must have taken personal command of this operation. Means it's more than what meets the eye."

"What do you make of it? What's going down?"

"Don't screw up. That's what I make of it." He had the binoculars to his eyes and was studying the horizon, moving them slowly from right to left and then back again, meticulous as he did all things.

Mark had not answered my question, so I knew something was troubling him. As a child he'd go silent when he didn't immediately know the answer, working through it internally.

Then the glasses stopped moving and, after a few more seconds, he said, "There they are, right where the radar shows them. See?"

He handed me the glasses. I couldn't see a thing other than sky and water. Mark reached for the radio, keyed the mike and said, "Station Corpus, this is UTB 303."

Almost instantly the reply came, the same voice as before, "Station Corpus, go ahead UTB 303."

"Visual confirmed. There are three vessels. Range three point two five nautical miles. Look to be fishing vessels. Can't tell the nationality, no flags."

"Proceed to the middle vessel. Do not board. They may be hostile. Accept cargo for transport if they provide it. You will be met at Station SPI. Code R2. Repeat Code R2. Acknowledge."

"Acknowledge. Do not board. Code R2."

"Confirmed. Out."

"UTB 303 Out."

"Man of few words," I said to Mark, as he continued to peer straight ahead.

"He said more than you might think. The victim is dead, or it's a diversion. There is a possibility of underwater activity, possibly hostile."

"All that from the message?"

"Code R2 is a possibility of submarine activity. Definitely something is going on. Also, a few minutes ago, I heard from UTB 310; that's the dispatch just before ours. The one Radioman Smith took. He's on station where the vessel taking on water said he was. Nothing out there. No sign of lifejackets, wreckage, nothing. Air surveillance has been called, but unless I'm mistaken, it'll turn out to be a diversion."

"Diversion?"

"They know how many people are on duty, and they know we won't dispatch unless at least two men are available. They had us send what they thought was the last craft on a wild goose chase. Didn't count on this one."

"But they called it in," I said in surprise. "Why do that if they don't want you to respond?"

"My guess is they wanted air rescue. Don't know why, but that's why the Captain held Helo 2. Someone's playing with us."

"Submarines? That usual in the Gulf?"

"That's classified. It may not be submarines; it's too shallow for normal operation. Maybe someone diving, doing something down there. In a few minutes, we'll slow and use the sonar. It'll tell us if anything's in the area. The good news is that the private fishing vessels are friendly. Or at least they should be."

"I'm not armed. You got weapons aboard this boat?"

"Of course. You're still licensed, right?"

"Yep, what do you have?"

"Here, keep watch and I'll get us fixed up proper."

In a few minutes, he was back and handed me a forty caliber Sid-Sauer P229R. He set a box of ammunition on the console and began loading his weapon. "You ever use one of these?" he asked.

"More important, have you?"

"On the driving range. Don't get much call for it in this job. But we're prepared when need be."

"Wish I could say the same." I nodded toward my shoulder, "This is the weapon that did the damage."

"Does that mean you've fired this before?"

"Trained with it. We're old friends."

"Get ready, I'm slowing down. You'll be able to see them very soon. I'm coming up on them out of the sun so they'll have trouble seeing us, unless they have radar going."

"I thought all boats had radar."

"These guys try to save every buck they can. Even if they have it, they'll save electricity by keeping it off as much as possible. Saves them from running the generator that much longer. This is a cutthroat business, if they're really fishing boats."

As predicted, the silhouette of three boats, each about a hundred fifty feet long, appeared off the starboard bow. They were moving slowly away from us. Mark steered for the center boat, and we were less than a hundred yards off their port side before I detected activity on their deck directed to us.

Mark spoke into the radio, simply saying, "UTB 303 on station. Time fourteen-twenty five. They know we're here."

Again, the reply was instantaneous. "They have not answered our calls for fifteen minutes. Approach with caution."

"Acknowledged."

"Roger, Out," came the terse reply.

Mark turned to me. "Did you get the ship's name? I couldn't read it."

"Couldn't read it either. Seems to be faded," I replied, squinting hard, but reading nothing.

When we were a few yards away, Mark picked up the microphone, flipped a switch on the console, and said, "Fishing vessel,

Fishing vessel, this is the US Coast Guard coming along your port side." The words bounced off the hull of the fishing boat and echoed back at us. He was using the electronic hailer.

Two men in fishing aprons gestured wildly in our direction.

I said to Mark, "I'm no seaman, but the way I read this is they want us to leave."

"That they most certainly do. Be careful, these guys can be nuts at times." He repeated his previous message and asked them to throw him a line.

"Go away!" a husky voice shouted from the other boat. "Not your business!"

"Request permission to come along side."

"No! Go away!" came the response.

"I must speak to your Captain," Mark barked, his command voice on display.

"No! Get away from here!"

"What is the name of your vessel? Where is she registered?"

"Get away! We are not in US waters. You have no business here."

"This water is patrolled by the United States Coast Guard," Mark responded, sounding very official. "It is most certainly our business. I must speak with your Captain immediately."

"No! Go away!"

I tapped Mark on the shoulder and pointed to the rear of the fishing boat where a man stood with a rifle pointed directly at Mark's head. "Better do as he says. Unless you want me to take him out. Even in this rolling sea I have a good angle."

"Not a good idea. You and me taking on these guys won't cut it." He slid the engine in reverse, and we gradually dropped back.

Mark tried again, this time from twenty yards out, "I must speak with your Captain. Do you have cargo for me?"

We could not hear the response, but the hand gestures were unmistakable.

Mark was on the radio reporting our situation, and when he finished, he said, "We're to stand off at the edge of visibility and wait for orders."

We slowly drifted back away from the three vessels, until they again vanished over the horizon. We didn't have to wait long. Mark took the call and his face dropped when we were ordered back to Station.

"What was all that about?" I asked when we turned for home. "Happen often?"

"Never to me. Seems that something else is brewing, or they would have dispatched some serious help. It's not our policy to back down when challenged. We'll probably never know what's going on, until we read about some big bust in the paper."

Mark did not say much to me on the way back to base, but he spent a lot of time with the headset on and talking into the microphone. It was obvious he didn't want to share his conversations with me.

FOUR

oming in toward land, the visibility cleared dramatically, and the entire inhabited five-mile stretch of the City of SPI made a spectacular view. I could see the surf breaking on the beach and dark dots, which I took to be people, in the waves and spread out along the sand.

At one point, Mark slowed the patrol boat and headed in as close as he could, and we worked our way south, just outside the breaking waves. I could make out a few surfboarders, but mostly people were bobbing and bodysurfing, as the small waves broke over the sand bars.

Mark pointed, "There are three sand bars between here and the beach. See there where the surf is breaking? That's where the outer edge of each bar is. You can stand on each one of them, but it's between five and six feet deep between them."

"That doesn't sound all that difficult then to swim out this far."

"Not at all, but you do need to watch for the rip tides. They can pull you down if you aren't careful. Every year, several people, usually folks with a bit too much beer in them, drown."

A moment passed. "You're staying at the TIKI, right?"

When I nodded, he continued, "That's it right over there."

"I wouldn't have recognized it from this view point," I said, and then, seeing something that unfortunately I did recognize, I pointed to an area of the beach just north of the TIKI. "Police action going down by the TIKI."

Mark immediately turned the patrol boat around and headed north, moving in as close as he could. The boat was rocking from side to side, and I had to hold on. Mark glanced toward the life jacket. "Put that on if you don't mind."

"We can swim from here if need be. No need for the jacket. Or walk even."

"Please put it on. I don't need to be answering any questions if you fall overboard."

I reluctantly pulled the jacket over my head and was about to make some smart-assed comment when he spoke again.

"Looks like an accident or possibly a fight, but fights are actually rare. This is one of the most peaceful beaches I've ever been around. Maybe a drowning, but they're mostly at the south end of the island, not up here. We'll hang here in case we can help."

While we watched, two other police vehicles, their red and blue lights flashing, turned onto the beach from the street next to the TIKI. That street, as far as I could see, was one of the few, maybe the only one that actually extended all the way to the beach. I could hear sirens over the sound of the surf, even though the wind was blowing inward toward the land.

Within a few minutes, several small fire vehicles turned onto the beach and moved north across the sand to join the group already there.

Mark slowed the boat even further. "This craft can be taken onto the beach, but we can't get over the bars with the tide this low. So there's not much we can do."

The radio sounded, Mark put on his earphones, said a few words into the mike, clicked off, and said to me, "Not good. A body washed up on the beach."

"One of the drunks get caught up in too much party time?"

"Not likely. His neck's been cut."

FIVE

Hours later, when I tried to return to my room at the TIKI, I was stopped at the end of the street by a police barricade.

"Street's closed," announced the woman inside the police uniform. "Can't let you through."

"What's going down?" I asked, knowing I'd get no real information.

"It's closed. Go up the beach to the County Park or turn around and go down the beach. Now get moving."

I thought of flashing my State Trooper shield, but it was back in Austin with my weapon. I reminded myself I was on leave. "How about if I park over there and walk. My room's in the TIKI."

"I can see that by the pass on your windshield. If you can find a place off the road, go ahead. But stay away from the beach."

"Will do," I responded, wondering how long I'd be able to curb the investigative urge cultivated by over twenty-five years of poking around crime scenes. This was not my business, I reminded myself for the umpteenth time since leaving Mark. I was not sure the admonition was taking hold. Mark had remained uncharacteristically quiet on the way back to the station. When we had arrived at the dock, he simply said, "Thanks for joining me today. We'll reset the meeting with Trich. I'll call you." He turned and disappeared into the building.

I had been dismissed.

I took a nap, woke, saw it was after seven, changed into my bathing suit, grabbed a towel and headed to the beach.

If I hadn't seen it earlier, I would not have known anything had happened. Children were running in and out of the surf, their watchful parents standing along the shore or sitting in ankle-deep water.

I focused my attention north, estimating the area I judged to be the center of the earlier activity. I saw what appeared to be four sticks coming out of the sand and standing about five feet tall. No one was within the boundaries circumscribed by the sticks.

I walked up the beach and then saw that the policewoman I had encountered earlier was now standing near one of the sticks. "What's up," I called to her as I approached.

"You again," she responded. "Told you before, police action."

"What kind of action?" This had all occurred in plain view of dozens of people. There was nothing private about it. "I mean, what's going on?"

"Nothing now."

"Earlier?"

"You got a reason to know?" she asked, her eyes coming alert.

"Curious is all."

"Man found dead over there." She pointed to the area bounded by the sticks. "You staying at the TIKI?"

"Yes, that's what I told you earlier."

"I remember. What room?"

I told her.

She held out her hand in greeting, "I'm Angella, what's yours?" Her badge read, *Martinez*.

Actually, she was doing what she should have been doing, getting identification of everyone around. She glanced at my bathing suit and thought better of asking for a photo ID.

"I'm Jimmy Redstone."

"What happened to your shoulder? Skiing accident?"

"I wish. Injured it at work. I'm here rehabbing it."

"With Teran? He's good. Get you back in shape if anyone can. He have you kayaking yet?"

"He's working me hard, but it's coming along. How long you plan to guard the sticks?"

"High tide'll wipe this clean. The pathology team is due any minute."

"The water's wiped it clean already."

My comment sparked her curiosity. Her eyes narrowed in thought before she replied. "Sand's funny. Looks spotless on the surface but a whole community is hidden down there. They'll scrape the surface and study it at the lab. What's it to you?"

I deflected the question. "They always do this for a drowning?" I knew it was a murder, always is when the neck's been cut. I wanted to see how she'd respond. Also, to tell the truth, I was enjoying the company of Ms. Martinez. She was easy to look at even when her intense brown eyes drilled into me. I guessed her to be in her late thirties and judging from her well-proportioned body she must have been spending time in the gym.

"Didn't drown. Could be an accident, don't know yet." She glanced over my shoulder. "Better be getting along. Team's coming up the beach now."

I turned and sure enough two jeep-looking vehicles were approaching, blue and white lights alternating on their bumpers.

I didn't immediately move from where I was standing and Officer Martinez took a step toward me.

"Okay, okay. I'm a *Bones* fan," I said, referring to the popular TV show. "Don't miss an episode. Curious what's going on that's all. I'll get out of the way."

"Personally, it's *CSI* for me. You want to, you stand over there." She pointed to a location near the water. "Nothing closer, you understand?"

"Got it." I walked to where she pointed, spread my towel, and plopped down. I had witnessed this scene countless times and was curious as to how thorough they were going to be with a crime scene that was deteriorating by the minute. After all, this was a resort town, not Austin or Houston.

They started by methodically spraying the sand with luminal spray and, not surprisingly, I didn't notice any tell-tale glow under the light. After all, I had to assume the saltwater would have washed the blood from the corpse long before it washed up onto the beach. However, checking still made sense.

Then they followed along with what looked like a metal detector. I concluded this was a particle detector that indicated where in the sand certain materials might reside. I had read about this gadget, but had never actually seen it used. I was impressed.

Every few feet, the technicians would read something on the small screen and then dig up the sand a foot in each direction. They carefully placed the sand in a plastic bag labeled with a tag printed directly from the detector. I wondered if the printing included a GPS location identification. At least they would be able to recreate the beach area at a later date if necessary.

I was impressed with their dedication and careful work habits. This team had been carefully trained. Maybe they were also *Bones* fans.

I eventually went back to my room and dressed for dinner—shorts and a T-shirt was the dress code on the island. It was now dark out and the forensics team was still busy on the beach. If nothing else, they were hardworking.

Earlier, Mark had mentioned an Italian restaurant, *Gabriella's*, he claimed was excellent. "Everything cooked fresh to order. You can eat at the bar, if you like, or sit in the dining room. It's decorated like a backyard with laundry hanging out to dry," he had said. "Also, if you want a place a bit upscale, but also excellent, I suggest the *Sea Ranch*. That's just down the road from the Station. Or you can try *The Big Donkey*. It's neat."

I decided on *Gabriella's*, and found a seat at the bar located just inside the door. I couldn't see any laundry hanging anywhere, positioned as I was directly in front of the big-screen TV. The Rangers were playing the Pirates in a tie game bottom of the ninth, two out. The Pirates were at bat and a runner was on second. I was the only person seemingly paying any attention to the game. Every conversation I could hear focused on the dead body. Consensus was that it was a white male, mid thirties, killed somewhere offshore and his body dumped from a boat.

This last bit of information, imparted by the bartender, a woman about my age, with skin that would have made an alligator proud, gleaned from the fact that no one was reported missing. I refrained from replying that an alternate hypothesis could be that whomever the victim came to the island with could have had reason to leave anonymously. Foul play usually gives rise to such non-civic behavior.

Also, the body could have been dropped from an aircraft, or from one of the many parasailing excursions we had seen earlier in the day. Focusing on a hypothesis at such an early stage is helpful in developing facts, but it's dangerous because it leads to non-development of other facts. Keeping an open mind sounds easy, but is perhaps the toughest lesson a good investigator must learn. Not that the bartender had any pretension of being anything other than a bartender—or perhaps a surfer.

"You new to the Island," she asked, as she removed glasses from the rinse water and began drying them. The leathery skin on the backs of her hands folded and unfolded as she worked.

"Been here a week," I answered her.

"Oh, you must be the guy working at the gym. Now that I think about it, your left shoulder does droop a bit."

"Word gets around this place pretty fast," I replied, "better watch myself."

"Small place really. Many folks workout at Teran's. Can't surf every day, got to keep in shape somehow."

"I haven't seen you there."

"Go in the afternoons just before work. Bet you're a morning person."

"Seems I'm there all day. Gone by noon, however."

"How's it coming along?"

"A bit more motion. Teran's working on it."

"If anyone can fix you up good, he can. Hey, speaking of surfing, I hear they found Wes' surf board abandoned on the beach about an hour ago."

"Who's Wes?"

"A local surfer. World class."

"What do you make of it?" I wasn't following why this was news, or even gossip.

"Wes doesn't surf at night, none of us do. And he wouldn't just abandon his board. A board's part of you, that's our lifeblood. Something's wrong."

"In what way is something wrong?"

"Don't know. But what with the body and all, it's spooky. Now Wes' board."

"How do you know it's his?"

"I didn't personally see it, but the person who found it knows Wes' board. I trust it's his."

"Where's Wes?"

"Who ever knows where he is? Got a place over on the bay, but don't know."

"Anyone check?"

"Not my department. Want a refill?"

"No, I'm heading home."

"Where's that?"

"TIKI."

"Oh, up by where the body was found." She looked at me with a slowly growing recognition. I realized she was studying my face in case she was called upon to identify the stranger in town. Everybody loves to play detective.

SIX

At the gym the next morning, the talk continued to be about the body on the beach. No new news was available and the conversation centered on Wes' board and concern about Wes. I was busy working out and stayed mostly out of the conversation.

Around noon, I was finishing up on the stationary bicycle, when I heard a familiar voice behind me say, "Found Wes over by the TIKI."

I turned to see Officer Martinez, now in shorts and a halter top, a towel over her shoulder, talking to Teran. Obviously, she was here to work out. My earlier assessment had been right. She looked infinitely better out of uniform.

Teran asked, "Is he okay? Was he hurt?"

"Cleaning the pool on some property, the big pink condo, cross from the TIKI. Apparently, he does that every day during the summer, unless he's out surfing. Seems his board went missing yesterday, stolen from the back of his truck. He was happy to get it back."

"Any connection between the board and the victim?" I asked, using any excuse I could dredge up to get off the bike. I had once again complained to Teran that I had come to get my shoulder in shape and he was busy working on my legs and cardio. He again gave me his stock answer, "It's all connected one to the other. Gotta fix it all, if we have any chance of getting the shoulder right. That's why it didn't work for you back in Austin. They only worked on the shoulder."

Martinez turned to me. "You're like the bad penny, keep showing up," I saw no trace of a smile. Her eyes were set as hard as ever.

Teran said, "Cut him a break, Ange. Guy's okay."

"I didn't say he's not, but he keeps showing up in this discussion of the dead guy. Makes a person think."

"You brought it up," I reminded her. "You're the one discussing Wes."

"I said nothing about the dead guy. I just was talking 'bout Wes."

"Okay, so I did. Sorry."

"Your story checks out. You're at the TIKI."

"Dumb of me to tell you that and not be there if I was up to mischief."

"You'd be surprised what people say and do down here. Seems the closer they get to the beach the dumber some get."

"I suppose," I replied. Addressing Teran, I said, "See you in the morning."

"Go do some kayaking, do your shoulder good."

"I'll think about it," I said, quickly slipping out the door.

My cell was beeping when I got to the car. The icon said I had missed four calls from Lieutenant Contentus. I quickly hit the return call button and he came on the line immediately.

"What the hell you into down there?" he said by way of greeting. "You're on leave and a dead guy shows up on your beach. You know what's going on?"

I told him what little I knew. He listened quietly, which was not his normal style. When I finished, he said, "What I'm about to say is confidential, at least for now. I'm sorry to have to say this, but he's one of ours. One of our best! His name'll come out soon enough, but he was working undercover in Mexico on drug smuggling with INS. Was actively reporting back as late as mid-afternoon yesterday. We knew from his reports something big was going down this weekend, but we could not get confirmation. He was in the process of reporting a cargo transfer when he went silent."

"So, where do I come in?" I asked, hoping he would assign me to work on the case. He hadn't called me to get information he already had from other sources.

"Stay undercover. From what you told me, and from what I'm picking up, no one knows you're with the Rangers. Keep it that way. Nose around, see what you can find out, but at all costs, don't let them find out you're with us. That clear?"

"That's not easy down here. Everybody knows everybody's business. One of the local cops, a real looker named Angella Martinez already got me pegged as having too much interest in what's going on."

"Stay undercover. That's important. Keep a low profile."

Ever the practical guy, I asked, "What does this mean about my leave?"

"Nothing! This is a favor between you and me. As I seem to recall, you owe me a few as it is. Just keep your head down."

Having Lieutenant Miller Contentus owe you one was always a good place to me. He might be a hard ass when it came to running the operation, but he always protected the backs of his friends. I think that's why I got off from the shooting. People went the extra mile for him. So I simply remarked, "I don't have my gun or shield. I'm naked, so I can't get too far out front even if I wanted."

"Can't see as to how you'll need either at this stage. Just as well."

"I'll do my best," I replied.

"Report to me personally when you have anything. Don't be getting out front, this is a quiet operation—and unofficial."

I didn't like the odds. But it was as close to active duty as I had been in two years, and I felt the adrenalin working already. And it felt good. "I'll call when I have anything," I said.

"Listen, just remember you're on leave, so you have no official cover. Just report back, no intervention or overt investigating."

"With both hands tied behind my back, who needs rehab on my shoulder?" I replied.

Contentus didn't appreciate the humor. "Keep your nose clean, you understand. This is a multi-jurisdictional issue, and tempers may flare a bit. Watch yourself. Report to me and no one else. You understand that?"

"Clear as could be, Lieutenant. Clear as could be." In fact, my instructions could not have been less clear. The Lieutenant could actually get more intelligence about what was going on by asking the bartender, or Teran, than by asking me. But I worked for him and they didn't. It would be my ass he busted if something went wrong. And he would bust it big time if I disobeyed him.

On the way back to my room, I saw a guy cleaning a pool across the street. His skin belonged to the same alligator family as that of the woman bar tender the night before. Sun baked and leathery. I strolled over to him. "You, Wes," I asked, my head peering over the pink-painted wall surrounding the pool. He held a long pole in his calloused hands.

"Ya, who wants to know?" A pleasant voice with no trace of hostility.

"Names, Jimmy. Heard talk you lost a surf board."

"Found it. Stolen from my truck Sunday." He nodded toward a white pickup with an open bed parked in an off-street parking area next to the wall where I was standing. "Found it on the beach last night."

"Any idea who took it?"

"Nope. Never happened before. Nobody bothers anything here. It's a bit banged up, nothing serious. Probably some kids fooling around."

"May I look at it?"

"Sure, but what's it to you? Just a surf board."

"Mind if I look?"

"Be my guest."

I examined the board, having no clue what I was looking for and not even knowing exactly how surfboards worked. Wes was right, the board seemed fine, and as I slipped it back onto the truck, it caught on the floorboard. I had to lift it over a ridge.

That caught my attention. I pulled it back out and examined the board more carefully. On each side edge about midway down the board, there were deep indentions as though someone had tied something onto the board and winched the binding tight against the sides. The grooves were not deep enough to have been made with a rope. I wanted to ask Wes about them, but if I did, the news would spread around the island and be traced to me immediately. I took several pictures with my cell phone. I thanked Wes and went to my room.

An hour later, I was ready for lunch so I changed into my bathing suit, pulled on a T-shirt and walked up the beach to the County park area, had a hot dog and a beer and started back. Several Constable cars were stopped on the sand, and uniformed officers were talking to bathers. My assumption was they were canvassing to take statements from anyone who had witnessed yesterday's events. I wondered why they hadn't done this yesterday.

One of the uniforms came over to me and said, "Pardon me, Sir, would you mind answering a few questions?"

Of course I said I'd be happy to answer anything they cared to ask. He then adjusted a paper on his clipboard and began working down the list of prepared questions. He began with my name, address, both local and permanent, and occupation. I toyed with what to answer and decided to simply say, "State employee, clerical." He didn't press further and I didn't volunteer.

"Where you on the beach yesterday between noon and five PM?"

"No."

"Did you by chance see the body on the beach?"

"Yes."

"Where were you when you saw the body?"

"On a boat out in the Gulf."

"What time was that?"

"Approximately two, maybe as late as three."

"What did you see?"

"I saw police and fire vehicles moving on the beach and stopping about there..." I pointed to the area within the stakes. The tide was in and a portion of that area was now covered with water.

"What was the occasion of you being out there on a boat?"

"A friend, actually the son of friend, asked me to go out with him for a few hours."

"Was that a fishing boat?"

"No."

"A sail boat?"

"No."

"Then what kind of boat where you on?"

"A Coast Guard boat."

"A what?"

"A Coast Guard boat."

"What were you doing on a Coast Guard boat?"

"My friend's son is the commander at the station here on the Island. He took me out for a few hours to show me around." There was no point in talking about the mission we were on. Had I mentioned the man with the rifle on the fishing boat I might still be there answering questions. That is, if the Coast Guard didn't shoot me first.

"That's most unusual. What's his name?

"Lieutenant Marcus Cruses."

"And you say you saw nothing?"

"Only what I've told you."

"Anything else you wish to tell us or you think we should know?"

"Nothing. Only that I thought the body was found in the City of South Padre Island. Why are you investigating? You're County, right?"

"We're County. We both have jurisdiction. And it's not exactly clear that the body was found within the City limits. Part of that area is County maintained."

"I see," I answered, wondering how in the world they would ever get to the bottom of this if jurisdiction became an issue. I was beginning to wonder if my boss had told me all that I needed to know.

"Have you identified the body yet?"

"We're not at liberty to discuss those matters. Thank you for your cooperation. If you think of anything further please call us." He handed me his card.

I walked down the beach toward the TIKI and sat looking at the water. There certainly is a soothing effect as the surf runs up and back against the sand, belying the contentious juncture where the two meet, the water continually battering and ripping at the shoreline and often at the people who inhabit the interface.

"Hey there," a friendly female voice addressed me, "returning to the scene of the crime, I see."

It was Officer Martinez, now in a bathing suit and carrying a beach towel. I again marveled at the woman's marvelous figure. She was someone I could be interested in getting to know better. "This your day off? I didn't expect to see you out here."

"Mind if I sit here or would you prefer to be alone with your thoughts? Teran said you're a good guy so I'll take him at his word."

"It's a free beach. Can't stop you." I laughed to show I was joking and motioned for her to spread her towel. "I assume you're not on duty under cover, so to speak, are you?"

"Just enjoying the beach. Come here every chance I get." She busied herself, placing her towel exactly where she wanted it. She smoothed out the sand under the towel and sat down. "I thought you said you were going kayaking."

"Teran wants me to kayak. Actually, I'm here for that purpose, but I can't seem to get it all together. Frankly, don't know how," I confessed.

"Well, I do. I'm up for it if you are. How about a little later? We can borrow one of Teran's and take it over to the bay. Can't launch it here, need real skill to do that. Surf will knock us about. Give me some time to swim and work on my tan. That okay with you?"

And to think I had been assigned to this gig. In the line of duty, this was working out well. I sensed a happy ending to the story. "That'll work just fine," I said. "I can use a bit of sun myself."

"I'm going in the water now," she said, jumping up from the towel and running across the sand. "Last in," she called over her shoulder, issuing a challenge she knew I could not refuse.

Like a teenager, I ran behind her but couldn't catch up until we were waist deep. She dove under a two-foot breaker that caught me in the chest and knocked me backward a half step. "Surf's a bit more robust than normal for July, but nice," she yelled. "Earlier in the year the water's clearer; this is kicking up sand."

That could explain why no one saw the body wash ashore. I started to say something but held my thought. I didn't want to spook her if I could help it. There would be time enough later for getting the information I wanted.

We swam; actually, we body surfed the waves for a while and then sat on the beach allowing the warm air to dry us.

I fell asleep on my towel, the sun's heat dissipated by the cooling breeze blowing off the Gulf.

I jumped when her hand touched my shoulder, not from pain, but from the sheer pleasure of her fingers on my skin. It had been a long while since anyone had touched me.

"Sorry to wake you, but our kayaking appointment will have to wait. My time-off's been cancelled. Got to report to the station."

"What's up?" I asked, trying to sound unconcerned.

"They found another body. We never have trouble, not this kind of trouble, and now two bodies in two days! All leave's been cancelled."

"On the beach? Where?"

"No, this one's in an apartment. Called in by a friend who found him."

"Not a drowning then."

"Not on the sixth floor. Gotto go. I'll call you at the TIKI when I'm free."

SEVEN

"**Y**ou're certainly well plugged in," Contentus quipped when I called with the news of the latest victim. Apparently, that information hadn't yet been released to the public, but all instances of suspicious death were immediately reported to the State Police. I then explained about my chance encounter with Martinez, and he replied, "Don't be too certain that was random."

I wondered if that was casual banter or whether he was sending me a message. While we were talking, I heard his keyboard working in the background. After a few moments, he said, "It's a bit of a mess down there right now. County believes they have jurisdiction over the body on the beach. The City is investigating, the Department of Homeland Security has made serious inquiries, and of course, the Drug folks are very much involved. Oh, and by the way, case you're interested, Martinez's husband filed for divorce a few months back."

"Thanks for the news," I replied, "and why is that important for me to know?"

"First words out of your moth were that she was a looker. Just thought you might want me to run a little background on the lady. Good record. Rather new to the job. Does what she's told. Keeps her nose clean. Bright."

"Thanks. So what do you want from me?"

"More of the same. Since we know the County has been canvassing witnesses I'll get copies of their reports."

"Won't that cause suspicion?"

"They'll think it's because of the multi-jurisdiction. We often do that in these types of cases. In fact, I believe they may have already filed the reports with us. Hold it, let me check."

He was gone about five minutes and when he came back, his voice was less passive than before. "Jimmy, you being on the ground there may have paid off already. Coincidences don't happen this way. The new dead guy's name is on the immigration watch list. He's an Ensign in the Coast Guard."

"What else do we know? Wait, what's a Coast Guard guy doing on the watch list?"

"Good point. I'll run it down. We know not much else. Looks to be an OD. Preliminary report is accidental."

"By the way, can you tell from the reports where the body, I mean the one on the beach, was first spotted?" This was a question I had been angling to ask Martinez when the time was right. I thought it strange that no one at the bar the night before had been talking about seeing the body float in or bobbing in the surf. That was exactly the kind of gathering where every imaginable scrap of knowledge is traded around like good weed.

"Everyone says they first noticed the body on the beach."

"How the hell does a dead body not get noticed until it's on the beach?"

"Beats me," Contentus said in the voice he reserves for washing his hands of a problem. "That's your job."

"Talk to you later," I responded and hung up. What I had wanted to ask was how the hell I was supposed to do my job with no badge and no authority. And with no one finding out I was peeking. But that conversation would have gone downhill faster than a runaway bull.

EIGHT

"Want to catch a late dinner?" It was Angella's voice on the phone about eight-thirty that night. "I feel bad for standing you up for kayaking earlier, but the job unfortunately comes first. Not much open now, but we can get burgers. I can meet you at *Louie's Backyard*. Know where that is?"

I had been hoping she would call, but hadn't counted on it. "See you in ten," I said, not sure whether the excitement I felt was for her as a woman or for her as a source of information. A bit of both I concluded.

She was in uniform when I arrived and sitting at a table overhanging the bay. The setting sun was hanging in the sky behind her. "Don't stand," I said as I approached the table, realizing as I said it that she had no intention of standing to greet me.

"I'm beat," she apologized. "Been on my feet since I left you. I suppose you might have eaten already, but I'm starved."

"As a matter of fact, I only had a bowl of soup. This is perfect."

We both ordered hamburgers. I had a beer and she drank a coke. "I make it a habit never to consume alcohol in uniform," she unnecessarily explained.

In an earlier day, I would have made some foolish comment. But instead, I replied, "I suppose that's a good habit to have, but I'm sure it gets in the way every now and again."

"Not as much as you might think."

We chatted back and forth. I wanted to ask about her personal life, find out about her hobbies, her family, what happened between her and her husband, but to do so would invite reverse queries. Until I was prepared to talk about my ex and myself, I needed to keep the conversation on neutral ground.

When the food arrived, we ate in silence, until I said, in a tone meant to convey ultimate non-interest, "So, what's going on? I'm curious about the new victim."

I hadn't fooled her in the least. She examined my face carefully, concern deepening in her eyes, the deep brown becoming even deeper as she continued to study me. Then, as if a switch had been operated, her eyes regained their brightness, and she said, "Canvassed the entire building. No one heard or saw anything. From what I could glean from talking to anyone and everyone, he had been alone since early morning when the guy he was staying with left for work. Vic apparently died of an overdose. Most likely cocaine, but won't know until the tox report."

"Who was he?"

"Name's not been released. He's a visitor to the island and staying in the apartment of his friend. That's who found him. Came home for lunch and there he was, sprawled on the living room floor. Friend lives here, teaches up north somewhere. Works in a bookstore here on the Island, a neat place called *Paragraphs On Padre Boul-*

evard, for the summer. Hey, I didn't get you out here to talk shop. So what do you do?"

"Work out."

"Stop toying. I mean back in Austin. How'd you injure your shoulder?"

"Fell off a truck. I work for the State." Remembering what I told the County cop, I added, "A desk job mostly, but sometimes I get out on the road."

"From the looks of it, you'd do better indoors."

I laughed and told her she was right about that.

The fun in her eyes had returned. "Look, I was serious about kayaking. John and I, John is my soon to be ex, did a lot of kayaking. I miss being on the water more than I'll ever miss that creep. I'm off Friday, assuming this doesn't get in the way. Thought we'd go then."

"I'd love it. What do I need to bring?"

"Nothing, just meet me at the gym at, say, noon."

"That'd work," I said, swallowing the last of the hamburger. "These burgers are surprisingly good. Must have mostly beef in them."

"What the blazes do you expect in hamburgers?"

"Some places seem to mix in old phone books. Actually, they mix a little meat to the moldy paper."

"Stop it. You need to select your places with more care." She flashed a quick smile, but the fatigue lines around her eyes were winning the battle. "I'd better go now, I'm exhausted, and I work the early shift tomorrow." With that, she drank the last of her coke, leaned close as if she were going to kiss me goodbye, but instead patted my shoulder. She whispered, "I also make it a habit not to kiss men when I'm in uniform."

I wasn't sure if that was meant as a promise of things to come or simply a statement of fact. Before I could make a smart retort, she was across the room and out the door.

I sat for a few minutes contemplating the end game if she had indeed just left behind a calling card. My ego argued for the calling card, but my brain told me otherwise. There was no question we played off each other well, and I had a pang of regret that I had been unable to tell her I was also a cop.

A group of folks were gathered around the bar passing around anecdotes about today's events like hors d' oeuvres. I took my beer and joined them. "Hey," one of the women called to me, "you were talking with that policewoman, what's the latest on the murder?"

When I shook my head, she turned fully around on the bar seat to face me and, in doing so, had to put her hand on the back of a woman standing beside her to keep from falling. It was clear she had had more than one too many. When she regained her balance, she brushed her bleached hair from her face and continued, "Must be something the good cop told you. She was nosing around all day at the condo, talking to everyone."

"We didn't discuss it," I said, perhaps more forcefully than I had intended.

"So what did you two discuss?" she pressed. "Most important thing ever happened on this God forsaken island where nothing ever happens and the lady cop has nothing to say! All in a day's work! My foot, it's all in a day's work! More TV trucks here now than were here when Dolly tore us a new one last year. Darn near wiped us out."

"Joy, now take it easy," interjected the woman whose back had been used to steady her. "Just maybe the man doesn't want to tell us what he knows. That's his right you know. Not everyone is into gossip." She turned to me. "Tell her to mind her own darn business."

"Gossip, my foot!" Joy retorted. "With a little help, maybe we can solve this thing. Maybe it's a serial killer!"

"Joy," her friend said, "one person died. Can't be a serial killer!"

"You don't know what you're saying! Serial killers always start at one. What you think, they start at four or five? You're naive that's what you are. Besides, it's two dead, but who's counting!"

"Guy dies of an overdose is one thing, guy dies on a beach is another. You're adding apples to peaches."

Joy then pointed directly at me and said at the top of her drunken voice, "Maybe he's the serial killer! How do you know he's not the one? See the way he holds his arm funny, got something to hide, you ask me."

"That's enough, Joy," said an older man sitting next to her at the bar. He stood and moved to take her arm. "We need to be going now."

I turned to face her. "What makes you believe he was killed? I understand he died of an overdose."

"Overdose my foot! That kid didn't drink, and he stayed away from drugs."

"You know him well?" I asked, certain that Joy had something on her mind she wanted to get out.

"What's it to ya? You got the dope from the lady cop, you tell us."

"We didn't discuss it. Was he a friend of yours?"

"I'm just saying he didn't drink or do drugs, that's all I'm saying."

"And just how would you know that?" the man standing beside her asked. His tone indicated a concern. My guess was that the two of them were a team— husband/wife, boyfriend/girlfriend—and he now sensed she had wondered off the reservation.

She spun around, drained the remains of her green drink, and replied, "You're not my keeper! You don't know everything I do, so there!" She then threw her head back over her shoulder and I had the distinct impression that had she been wearing a scarf she would have tossed the scarf across her shoulder as well in an overblown attempt at drama.

"That's enough, Joy. You've had more than you can handle for one night." The older man now had a firm grip of her arm. "You're cut off, no more. We're going home."

Yanking her arm free, she replied, "You're the one who's cut off, buster. See how you like that!"

"Joy, I said we're going now." Clearly, his patience had worn thin. I surmised that he had played this scene often. "Take my hand so you don't trip."

She pushed his outstretched hand away, "I don't need no help from you or anybody. I can take care of myself. I'm fine." She turned to me. "He was murdered, I'm sure of it. He was murdered! It's a serial thing."

"Do you have evidence that he was killed?" I asked, hoping she would continue talking.

"Any simpleton knows if you don't drink and don't do drugs and you die from an overdose, you were killed! Even I know that! Are the cops stupid or something?"

"Some might draw that conclusion, but not all facts are in yet."

"You a cop? You talk like a cop!"

"Just an interested person, same as you."

"Same as me, my foot! You know what's going on! I don't! I'm scared. I saw you talking to the cop; you know something's wrong!"

Her escort interrupted, "He wasn't exactly hiding that fact. So what? You're always making mountains out of a little pile of dirt. Let it be."

"No," she shouted, pushing him back again. "He was at the beach talking to the County cops!"

If I hadn't been looking straight into her eyes I would never have seen it. It was the same look of terror that I've seen over and over when a suspect blurts something that he or she instantly regrets having said. For the briefest moment, Joy's eyes had filled with that same terror, the terror of being caught by your own words.

I tried to further engage her, but the fear had taken hold and she wanted away from me as fast as possible. She turned to her escort. "Let's get out of this place," she said. "Party's over. Take me home." With that, she took his hand and marched toward the parking lot.

"What was that all about?" I asked the woman she had been with.

"Never saw her like that. Joy loves to party, always upbeat and fun, but never drunk like that."

"Is she safe getting home? That her husband with her?"

"Not for long. She's fixin' to dump him. Man sponges off her. Been together for as long as I've known her. A good five years at least. She's the one with the money; he does nothing I can see. Takes lots of trips, says he's going hunting. Joy hates hunting. Who the hell knows what he's doing when he's off *hunting*."

"Each to his own, I suppose," I replied, wanting to focus more on Joy. "How does she know so much about the victim?" I was curious about the fright I had seen in her eyes and actually in her whole demeanor.

"Hey, maybe Joy was right. You a cop or something?"

"Curious, that's all. Everyone likes playing detective. Maybe solve a murder or something."

"So you agree with her, it was murder."

"Just saying. Following up on what she said. She seemed convinced. You have any feeling for why she's so convinced?"

My cell went off before I could follow up. It was Mark wanting
to meet me. I told him where I was, but considering everyone here
seemed to think I was a cop, I thought better of that. We decided to
meet at Denny's. Didn't expect any of the players in this caper to be
hanging out there at midnight.

NINE

Mark was waiting when I walked in, clearly agitated. "Homeland Security's going nuts," he blurted, even before I slid into the booth opposite him. I had to be careful not to catch my leg on the ripped vinyl seat.

"In what way?" I asked, trying to calm him while at the same time obtaining as much info as I could.

"You remember when we approached that fishing boat, I turned on the video cameras?"

"I saw you flip a switch."

"Well, I forgot that when we went to red alert the system automatically came on when the craft left the dock.

"I didn't remember to turn it off, but that didn't matter because, as I said, it would have remained on anyway. We actually have video of the people on the fishing boat and also of the shore line before and after the body was found."

I sat forward waiting for him to continue.

"I realized that a few minutes after we got back, so I retrieved the video file from the craft. Actually, I copied it to a flash drive and watched it on a station monitor. I saw something in the water just off shore, but that camera only captures what is out of the water, not what's under the water, so something, if it was anything at all, came in and out of the water."

"What was it? What did you see?"

"Can't be sure it was anything. So I uploaded the file to Corpus. They have equipment that can take those pictures apart and see anything out there."

"I take it something's amiss, or we wouldn't be having this conversation."

"I sent the file to Corpus. The file went missing. Every transmission of this nature is logged on the sending end and on the receiving end. It's not in the log at my station and the same with Corpus!" He paused, sipped his now cold coffee and continued, "I checked on it a few hours ago and that's when I learned it's not in either log."

"Not logged in. That, I assume, is serious. What have you done since you discovered that fact?"

"I went to the patrol boat so I could copy it again. These files are maintained on the original computer for at least a week, often longer." His normally rock-solid composure was gone. Pain showed on his face. "The originals were erased!"

"Is that unusual?"

"Here's what's troubling me. I'm the only person with authority to clear those files from the on-board computer."

"Then someone removed the files from the computer on board the patrol boat without authority."

"Exactly. At least not with my approval."

"Any thoughts as to who—or why?"

"Had to be someone up the command, because I'm the only person at the Station with the code for the computer."

"Who could have gotten on the boat to take the files?"

"That's it. I can't find anyone who was in place who had the proper codes." His command resolve faded, and he looked across the table at me as a son would look at a father, his eyes pleading for help. "This has never happened to me before. What should I do?"

"Beats me," I said, too hastily. "I don't think you have many options, not yet anyway. Are any other files missing?"

"Didn't think to look. That's a good idea. I'll check."

"I don't mean to tell you how to run your operation, but if you find any files of interest, copy them before you upload and save the copies. Get any copies you have to a secure location and don't carry them on your person. I assume it's not improper to make copies or you wouldn't have done it in the first place."

"So long as they're not stored off Station."

"I assume you still have the flash drive?"

"In a safe place."

"By the way, did you catch any flak about me being out there with you?"

"Nothing was said. You're with the Rangers. Why would anyone care that you were an observer? There's an operation going down, something to do with drugs in Mexico. I heard about it, but I have no details. The Gulf Coast Cartel from what I hear."

I debated sharing with Mark what I knew about the dead guy on the beach and decided it was better being upfront with him. If there was anyone in the world I could trust it would be this kid. "Keep what I'm about to tell you under your hat. The victim on the beach was a Ranger working undercover in Mexico with the DEA. There's a big operation on to put a crimp in the trade. I don't think for one moment the missing video is disassociated with his death."

Mark took in what I said, pondered a few moments, and then said, "That means the entire operation, I mean the fishing boats, the dead guy on the beach, and possibly that false sinking report are tied together."

"Most likely. And to add a twist, a guy turned up dead earlier today." I checked my watch, "Yesterday to be exact, of a drug overdose. Possibly connected."

"What's the connection?"

"He gave a statement to the County uniforms. I don't believe in coincidences, so in my book he's connected until proven innocent."

"So, you don't think I'm paranoid?"

"A little paranoia never hurt a good lawman. Just don't do anything foolish, like trying to solve the erased video file mystery. Leave it alone. Whoever erased it knew what the hell he was doing. You meddling won't sit well."

"I'll try to remember that, but it won't be easy."

"Treat it as an order. Leave it alone."

"Yes, Sir," Mark said, throwing a mock salute. "Thanks for taking time to talk with me. And thanks for the suggestion to check the other computers. I'll work on a time for you to meet Trich. You'll really like her."

Mark and I walked out to the parking lot together, and I watched as he turned south onto Padre Boulevard, heading back to the Coast Guard station. I turned north and headed toward the TIKI. I thought about the missing video file and it added another piece to the many unresolved pieces of this puzzle.

Then I thought about what he said about Trich. When somebody tells me I'll like someone, I'm never sure if they're trying to convince me—or themselves.

TEN

In the morning I was in the gym as I had been almost every day since I came to SPI. The hard work was beginning to pay off. The amount of weight I could move with my left shoulder and arm was steadily increasing.

My ex-wife always said that you can get information on anyone in town by hanging out at the hairdresser's. She was only half-right—the female half. Seems as though both halves find their way at one time or another to the Sweat Shop.

I found that out only too well when Joy came bounding through the door, the effects of her over indulgence the night before nowhere present.

I was in the back room working on my upper back muscles, using some God-awful contraption when she arrived. The contraption seemed to always be winning. At least with a human there was a chance your opponent might trip, catch a cold, faint, die, or even throw you a bone once in a while to humor you. Not so with the machines in this place. They were out to win at all costs, and the best you could do was count to some pre-ordained number and then stop. The machine didn't care what number you counted to. That was your problem, not its.

I had given the machines names, most of which were not flattering. When I heard Joy's voice, I doubled the count. The last thing in the world I wanted was to get into it with her.

"Hey, what's gotten into you today?" Teran asked, when he realized I had exceeded his count. "Usually, I can't get you to go the distance and today you're a man determined. Build up your delts. That's what you're here for. Come here, I want you to meet someone."

And that's when I was formally introduced to Joy Malcolm. "We met last night," she told Teran. "I'm afraid I was not awfully nice to your friend, now was I?"

"I've seen worse," I replied. "But it's not often I've been called a serial killer in public, I must admit."

"What was that about?" Teran asked, bewildered.

"Your friend, Joy, thinks there's a serial killer loose on the Island and she accused me of being that guy."

"I'm sorry," Joy said, throwing her hair back out of her eyes. "I'll just have to make it up to you, that's all. Any friend of Teran's has to be a friend of mine."

"You're assuming we're friends. I just train here." I turned to Teran, "Does that make us friends?"

"In here," he chided, "we're all friends. Only way it'll work. Joy, what's up with that serial killer thing? One person murdered, that's not serial."

"Two people."

Teran studied her as I had last night. "Guy in your building? He died of an OD. Nothing serial in that." He rolled his eyes in my direction.

"He was murdered! I know it, sure as I'm standing here." She turned to me. "I'm sorry I said what I did about you last night. Got out of hand. But I know I'm right. Not about you. I mean about the second murder."

I assumed she meant she was sorry for calling me a serial killer. "I've been called worse. But you had better be careful who you say things like that to. Get you in some trouble."

"Everybody knows I'm harmless. I make a lot of noise, but I'm harmless."

You drink too much, is what I wanted to tell her. Instead, I said, "So long as you're with friends that works. Gotta be careful, is all I'm saying."

"I owe you something for what I said. Kind of like a make-up lunch or something." She smiled broadly, her posture calculated to emphasize what was once a well-proportioned figure, but now had gone a bit to the wide-body side of comfortable. Surprisingly, however, in the fresh light of day and without discernable makeup, she gave off a softer, more inviting aura than she had last night when she was fully decorated. "Don't want to leave any hard feelings, now do I?"

"There's no need to make up anything. I'm not upset."

"But I am. I acted rude and not very lady-like. I want to show you I'm not like that, not at all. I want you to have a good impression of the people on this Island. This is a great place to live."

I did want to hear why she thought the OD was murder, so I said, "If you insist. Who am I to turn down an offer such as that from a friend? When and where?"

"How about *Naturally's*? It's all organic."

The thought of a sprout sandwich did nothing for me. But I was the guest and I could always catch a burger and fries later on. "See you then," I replied and retreated to the far back room to retrieve one of the large balls that always congregated in the far corner. Forty sit-ups stretching over the ball was my punishment for accepting her offer. After thinking about the burger and fries I craved, I added on another ten sit-ups for good measure.

Over lunch, Joy turned out to be much less of a ditz than the Joy who had been drunk in the bar the night before. In fact, she was rather serious over lunch. She explained that her marriage to John was long past its ending point, but her husband refused to acknowledge the fact.

"Listen, Jimmy," she confided, "I can't determine if he's staying because he truly loves me, or because..." here she paused, thought awhile, apparently trying to properly phrase what she was about to say, then said, "because I pay all the bills." Her voice dropped con-spiratorially low.

"Does he have any money?" I asked, certain I already knew the answer.

"He might have at one time, but doesn't seem to now, at least not that I can tell. When I met him, he had a condo on the beach and drove a nice car. That was about six years ago."

Joy paused to suck in a long breath before continuing. "My first husband died suddenly, ten years ago, heart attack, and left me some money. I moved down here to think, clear my head, start a new life. Then I met John. He was an investment banker, or so he claimed. Never seemed to go to work, but he spent a lot of time on the phone, so I naturally assumed he was conducting business. I later found out he was betting on anything that moved."

"I know the type," I commented.

"And apparently losing," Joy went on without breaking her train of thought. "One day, I came into his condo and he was on the phone yelling at someone, saying things such as, 'How dare you not pay on time,' and 'I'm about to be evicted because of late payments,' that kind of stuff. He went on and on berating the person at the other end of the line for not making payments on time. When I asked who that was, he said, 'My numb nuts father, that's who! The man was late with my condo and car payments. My car got repo'd and I'm about to get tossed from here!'"

"Don't tell me, let me guess," I injected. "His father stopped paying the rent on his condo and it's his father's fault that he was thrown out."

"And for the loss of his car as well."

"Did he ever tell you what happened to cause his father to stop paying?"

"Wouldn't discuss it. But truth is, I didn't believe him. He's not exactly a young man himself. Claims he's sixty, but I'm guessing more like sixty-five, maybe older. That would make his father, what, eighty, eighty-five?"

"About that. You ever met him?"

"No. He says since his father stopped his *allowance*, imagine, he calls being kept an *allowance*, he hasn't spoken to the man. May be dead now for all I know. I know nothing about his life, except what he chooses to tell me. He was married once and won't talk about it."

If I've learned anything in my years as a cop, it's that there's no limit on what women—or men for that matter—choose to do with their lives. I've investigated so many situations with what would normally be considered bizarre marriages that nothing surprises me anymore. There's simply no accounting for what people will do when romance, or even the thought of romance, intervenes. The ledger is bursting with otherwise wise and stable individuals who have fallen from grace over matters of the heart. I remained silent, waiting for her to tell me the inevitable conclusion.

"Suffice to say," she continued, "I came to his rescue and allowed him to move in with me. Oh, I loved him. The man is good..." she paused, "I'm telling you more than you need to know. I'm just say-ing he knows how to treat a lady. Let's leave it at that. We used to take long walks on the beach, great conversation. He knows about everything, and I felt alive being with him."

"So what's changed," I wondered out loud.

"For starters, he disappears a lot. Goes for what he calls, 'men's time away'. Hunting, fishing, that sort of thing. I don't really mind that so much, but he never stopped betting on the horses and sports. You name it; he's got money, my money, on it. I know the odds on everything going on in Vegas."

"How's he do?"

"Can't really tell. But he seems to be holding his own, maybe making some, because I never have to put any money in, except for one time I had to pay off debt. Since then he seems to have some walking around money."

"Can you blame him for not wanting you to leave? I wouldn't want you to leave either if you did that for me. Can't blame the guy, he's got it soft."

She studied me across the table for a moment, and then, her voice low and calm, said, "Jimmy, you'd never treat a woman that way. I've seen you in the gym and you look like you could pull a man apart if you wanted to, but you're a nice guy under it all. John is the opposite, he couldn't stand up to anyone, he's all for himself. Not a good bone in him."

"So, why's he still with you? Actually, then what's holding you back from showing him the door?"

"That's what I keep asking myself and I don't know."

I'd seen this story before, so what I was about to say wasn't pure conjecture; it had been written in her eyes the night before. "You were seeing the dead guy, weren't you?"

She sat back in her chair, moving as far from me as she could and still remain in the booth.

I leaned across the table and lowered my voice. "This stays between us. I'm right about you seeing him, that much I know. You can
tell me the truth."

She reached for my hand. "I do trust you. I can read it in your
eyes. I like you. You're honest. Oh, well, you guessed it anyway.
John and I haven't got it on for over six months now. He doesn't
seem to mind, just goes along with it. A few months back I thought
he was sneaking out, but all he was doing was trying to hide his
bets."

"What's the dead guy's name?"

"Heart."

"Heart?"

"Hardwick Janson Monroe. Went by Heart. Nice guy. A bit
young for me, though." When I didn't respond, she continued, "He's
mid-thirties. I got twenty years on him."

She looked at me, clearly expecting me to deny that she could
be mid-fifties. When I remained silent, she said, "You're not a wom-
anizer, are you?"

"I've said nothing and you came to that conclusion. I can't imagine what you'd be thinking if I actually said something."

"You're putting me on, you know. Having fun at my expense."

"I'm listening to what you've been saying and trying not to interrupt. You were telling me about Heart. How did you meet him
and when?"

"At the condo pool and on the beach. He was staying in our
condo."

"Is that where you two went when you were *seeing* him?"

"That's crude. I take back those nice things I said about you."

"I didn't mean it that way. Just trying to visualize your relationship with Heart."

"You got it right. We'd spend time on the beach, and then I'd follow him up to his place like a schoolgirl in heat. I told myself it was crazy, silly even, but there I was laying on the beach every day counting the minutes until he'd pick up his towel and disappear over the dunes."

"You guys drink, do drugs, what?"

"Nothing but sex. He was good. He wouldn't touch the alcohol and refused to allow me to have any. Said it did nasty things to your body. The man ate no meat; he was a vegetarian, a vegan really. Had me about convinced to give up meat. He even made me promise to not drink at all, even when I was not with him."

"Is that why you say he was murdered?"

"How can a person who worshipped his body, and he had a body to worship believe you and me on that, how could he OD on cocaine or on anything?"

I did agree with her on that point, assuming he was not lying about not taking drugs. "How can you be so sure he didn't do drugs? Just because he told you he didn't doesn't always mean it's true."

"It's true alright. His body was too perfect, his diet too controlled, for him to have lied. A woman knows these things."

"So, what's your take on it all?"

"Someone wanted him dead."

"Why? What did he do? Who was he?"

"Just a guy on vacation. Staying with a friend."

"What did he do for a living?"

"I'm not too good at getting this right, judging from my track record. He was a teacher like his friend, the guy he was staying with."

"What kind of teacher?"

"Coach, I think."

"What sport?"

She thought for a moment and then answered, "Basketball, I believe."

"Why? Why was he killed?"

"I'm not sure. I hadn't seen him that day which was unusual. It was Sunday and John and I went to breakfast. That was unusual in itself, because John never wanted to do breakfast. But he did that day, so we went across the bridge to a place called *Marchan's*. Great place. Police hang out there. Police chief eats there. It's part of the *White Sands* motel. John seemed to want to talk to me. I kept thinking he wanted to talk about our marriage, *what was wrong* type of discussion. But he never brought it up. Maybe he was waiting for me to say something. We didn't get back to the Island 'till after one, maybe close to two. I remember because I didn't want to miss Heart. I changed and went to the beach, hoping I hadn't missed him. He never showed up—or had already left—I don't know which."

"Then what did you do? Did you go to his place looking for him?"

"You *are* a cop, aren't you?" She again pulled back, this time her eyes hardened in anger.

I had gone too far and not in a very subtle way. Now my cover was about to be blown. I tried to deflect. "Just watch too many detective shows, like *Bones* and *CSI*. I'm just asking the natural questions."

"They seem too natural for you. Let's talk about something more pleasant."

"Like?"

"Like, what are you doing this afternoon. Let's do something fun."

"Like? You seem to be the expert on afternoon fun-time activities."

"Stop that! I really do take back all the nice things I said about you. That's uncalled for. I just lost my lover; I'm not ready for another—not yet anyway. I meant like parasailing over the bay."

"I'd love to," I said. And surprisingly, I meant it.

ELEVEN

I was physically exhausted when I finally returned to my room. The parasailing was excellent, giving breathtaking views of the bay. I swear I could see all the way to Port Mansfield, nothing but sand dunes on the Gulf side north of where the city ended. The sun and water had wiped me out, and I looked forward to a good nap on the beach and then dinner.

But it wasn't to be.

Officer Angella Martinez was standing outside my door when I emerged in my trunks, a towel over my shoulder. She was wearing shorts and a tank top and I had a hard time focusing on what she was saying. The woman was the very definition of hot.

"This an official call," I managed to get out when I gathered my wits.

"That depends," she answered, flashing a rare smile, "on your definition of official."

I knew that look. She wanted a favor in the line of duty, but the question was difficult to phrase. "Bet we both have the same definition. I assume this is official. Spit it out."

She did not immediately respond. I waited in silence.

Finally, she said, "You don't make anything easy do you? I have the feeling you always know what I'm about to do or say."

"A student of human nature, I suppose." Actually, simple. Been there done that. Seeing the movie a few times makes anyone appear smart.

"Okay, what am I about to ask you?"

"A favor, that much I know. Precisely what the favor is I don't know."

"I need your help. This is strictly business, so when I tell you what it is, don't get the wrong idea."

"Sounds suspiciously like it has something to do with spending time in my room. If that's it, the answer's yes. Rather, it's hell yes."

"You're something, you are. Never known someone so cocky sure of himself. But you're actually close. Just not your room. Actually, a tent up the beach."

"That's even better," I replied. My response sounded sarcastic, so I added, "I didn't know you could sleep on this beach. It actually does sound like fun."

"Can't on the town beach. But you can on the County part just up a ways."

"So, what's this about?"

"I don't usually get into this stuff. I'm a patrol cop not a detective or anything, but the Captain wants me to put my ear to the ground, see what's going down with the beach population. He thinks some drug deal's happening and wants me to mingle with the *tent folk* as he refers to the campers. I told him a lone woman just showing up would tip them off. He suggested I take along somebody from the department. Can't use any of the regular investigators, they know them all. The few guys they don't know would only lead to problems down the line I don't need."

"You mean there's no one in the department you could spend a night with in a tent."

"I'd never live it down. Spend a night or two in a tent with one of those guys and there'd be hell to pay."

"I understand only too well how that goes. Your Captain know you're taking me?"

"I told him about you, yes."

"What'd he say?"

"If he hadn't agreed, I wouldn't be here."

I smiled, wondering if her boss knew I was a Ranger. If he did, my phone would have been ringing with Contentus mad as hell at me.

"I see your mind working overtime," Angella injected, apparently mistaking concern over my boss for sexual machinations. "Now don't be getting any crazy ideas. This is not date night. You pull any funny business I'll shoot it right off."

I had no illusions that she was kidding.

"Be ready at seven," she instructed. "We'll cook on the beach. I'll bring everything we need. Courtesy of the city of SPI."

True to her word, at seven sharp, she pulled up in a jeep loaded with camping gear and coolers, several fishing poles standing upright from holders along the front bumper. In answer to my question as to how long she thought we'd be out, she answered, "Probably just tonight, but just being prepared, that's all. Nothing wrong with over supplying."

Off we went, turning onto State Route 100, which was the extension of the main road through town, and driving north about five miles. She turned right onto a hard packed sand trail that had a beach access number on it. We drove through an opening in the dunes and turned north at the water. We then followed the water for about fifteen miles, passing several camping areas where rows of tents and vans were lined up.

Eventually, as we moved north along the beach, the pockets of campers lessened, and the few who were there were spread out. Angella stopped the Jeep about halfway between two small groups and took out her binoculars. She studied the folks north of us who were barely visible to my naked eye. "That's who I was hoping to find. This will do nicely," she announced. "Got about two hours, maybe a bit less, of sunlight, so let's get the tent set up and cook dinner."

"Which one of these got the beer?" I asked, already poking among the coolers.

"That one," she said pointing to the largest of the three. "Go easy on the alcohol, it's mostly for show."

I popped open a Miller and said, "Want one?"

"Not now."

"Oh, I forgot, you don't drink on duty?"

"That's not what I said. I said I didn't drink in uniform."

"You're not in uniform now."

"Poor choice of words, I know, but I'm not ready. There's work to do."

"Seems we're having our first domestic argument," I teased.

She wasn't amused. "Do I have to do this alone or are you going to lend a hand," she called when the tent was half out of the Jeep.

"Give a guy a chance. I'll get the other end, but remember, we're out here to have fun—or at least give off the appearance of having fun—so don't run this like a military operation."

She forced a larger-than-life smile, "Just grab the tent and get on with it. I'm beginning to think I made a mistake."

We worked in silence for a while and, within fifteen minutes, we were ready to move in. I have to say, the prospect of sleeping in a tent this far from civilization, excited me. This promised to be an interesting night. The Jeep had been unpacked, and I realized there was not as much stuff as I had initially thought.

When I commented about lack of sleeping bags, she said, "We're on sand, remember. Don't need bedding, a sheet will do," She rummaged in a cooler, produced a couple of good-looking steaks. "Now I'll get the grill going. You change into your trunks and take that fishing rod and go catch us a fish."

"We'll starve to death if you rely on my fishing."

"That's what the steaks are for, but fishing will blend us in with everyone else out here. A friend of mine, a former Marine by the name of Mike, says the best fishing is with a metal spoon. I brought some shrimp, but try the spoon first. Just throw it out and bring it in slowly. Appearances are all that count. I wouldn't know what to do with a live fish even if you got lucky."

I took hope—probably false—from her *getting lucky* comment and trudged out into the warm surf. In fact, Angella was right about the fishing. Nothing was even nibbling. I could make out men from the groupings north and south of us standing on the second sand bar with fishing rods. Every now and again, I could hear human sounds but couldn't make out actual words. Between the wind and the waves breaking on the bars, I could not even communicate with Angella on the beach, let alone try to understand anything those men were saying.

I started in toward shore, took two steps, and a fish hit as I was reeling in the line. The fish, an elongated skinny one with a large mouth, was much too small to keep, so I turned back to show Angella what my efforts had produced, holding it up for her to see. To my surprise she was not in our camping area.

Thinking she was in the tent, I stood with my back to the surf, waiting for her to emerge, the fish struggling on the hook. When she didn't appear after what seemed like five minutes, but most likely was only about half that, I became concerned.

I started toward shore. Coming off the sand bar, the water rose to my shoulders and I realized that the tide was coming in because, on my way out, the water had only been waist high. I hadn't paid attention to the tides, and I wondered how much of a swing there actually was. I had visions of water covering us in the middle of the night and trapping us in that little tent. I had read stories of such occurrences along the northeastern Atlantic coast but, from my knowledge of the Gulf coast, tides were nothing to worry about.

Another step toward shore and the bottom fell away, my feet working frantically seeking bottom. Water filled my nostrils as I tried to paddle with one hand and hold the fishing rod over my head with the other.

A wave broke over my head and the taste of saltwater filled my throat. I considered abandoning the fishing rod so I could swim naturally, but the thought of explaining its loss to Angella overcame my impulse.

I tried to doggie paddle toward shore, but made little headway. The waves breaking over my head filled my mouth with seawater, and I coughed it out in what seemed a losing battle. I paddled as hard as I could and managed to keep from being dragged back out.

I was being carried northward and away from the beach by what I guessed to be a rip tide. The tent was now south of me and I was closer to the next campsite than I was to mine. Alarmingly, I was moving slowly, but gradually, out to sea.

I thought of trying to find the second sand bar, hoping I had not already been swept beyond it. I actually took several strokes in that direction before I realized that something was in the water not far from where I was swimming.

I tried to see what it was but it kept disappearing, only to reappear again a few seconds later.

The image of a shark flashed before me. Then I realized I was trailing the fish, the shark's natural dinner, and a shark might actually be following me.

Or had the shark already eaten the fish? If that was the situation, then reeling in the fish would only bring the shark closer.

Or was it out there circling in the shadowy water waiting for a good attack angle? I visualized the shark, its huge mouth open, exposing its sharp teeth as it prepared to sink into a tasty leg—or some other vital part of me.

I immediately let go of the fishing rod and swam as hard as I could toward shore, making little progress as the waves continued pushing me north. What lay beyond the next camp site I didn't know, but I did know that if I didn't get to shore soon, I might not have all my God-given body parts if and when I ever did make it.

Finally, my right toe touched sand. When I tried to stand, the sand gave way and my foot again hung suspended as my head sank under water. A wave broke overhead, and it was several seconds before I emerged, having involuntarily swallowed what seemed like half an ocean. My throat burned from the salt and I spit out what remained in my mouth. Lesson number one learned many years ago: Don't panic! Easy when you're in a swimming pool with instructors pacing along side, harder when you're alone with saltwater bubbling from your nose and there's no bottom to be found.

Another wave caught me, and my body rushed forward, my face again buried in swirling water. My left arm hit what I thought was the shark. The shark, lucky for me, turned out to be the sand bar. The next wave pushed me onto the bar and another wave broke over me, keeping me pinned on hands and knees. Something hit my legs, and I involuntarily pulled them up under me, certain that when I looked down I'd see my blood steaming into the Gulf of Mexico.

The water rushed out and I quickly pulled myself to a sitting position before the water again broke over my head. I glanced down and counted my toes like you would with a new-born baby. Finding all intact, I began working my way toward shore, pausing to catch my breath and checking to be sure there were no fins following me.

When I reached the middle bar, I could stand with the water at chest height. I recalled what Mark had said about there being three sand bars, and knew that there was one more to go before I reached shore. Slowly, I got my bearings and realized I was roughly parallel with the campsite Angella had been watching and about fifty yards offshore. The fishermen I had seen earlier were no longer in the water.

The sun had set, and what residual light there was allowed for silhouettes and shapes, but no details. I could hear voices but the surf still blocked the actual words.

I started in toward the beach and almost immediately stepped off the bar. Again the water rose, but this time it only reached to my chest. Here, the current was decidedly less. I trudged toward shore.

I stumbled when my feet hit the first sand bar, and I sat in the water listening to the sounds from shore. I realized one of the voices I heard was female and familiar.

It was Angella's voice and agitated, frightened even. I couldn't immediately understand what she was saying. Nor could I make out what the men were saying, but the exchange was agitated.

They were all talking in Spanish. This was a sound scenario all too familiar to me from many years of dealing with criminal activity along the border.

They were all focused on Angella, and I was certain no one had yet seen me. I slipped back off the sand bar and moved out farther to a point where my body was mostly underwater.

I floated in the surf listening, allowing my mind to concentrate on the criminal Spanish I knew, which was just enough to understand the drift and to communicate a few commands.

I heard a deep voice say, *"Tenemos música, un montón de peces. Estamos teniendo una fiesta en la playa."* My translation was something about music and plenty of fish and a festival in the water.

To which Angella replied, *"Es hora de ir. Mi hombre está esperando mi regreso"* I understood that to mean, her man was occupied. That didn't make sense. Maybe she was trying to warn them that she had a man looking after her.

"No se preocupe. Vamos a cuidar bien de tu hombre." This was followed by laughter and one man pushing another. My guess was that they had volunteered to take good care of me.

Angella turned and began walking back south toward our camp. The man who had been speaking to her grabbed her arm. *Una mujer sola aquí con un grupo de hombres no es seguro. Usted necesita protección.* The tenor of his voice was now one of hurt, as though she had dishonored him. To me, it sounded as though he threatened, or at least questioned, her safety.

"Voy a estar bien," she replied, pulling her arm from him. *"Gracias por el generoso ofrecimiento de los alimentos. Buenas noches."* That I understood. She had thanked him for the food and told him good night.

Two of the men started after her, and the first one shouted, *"Déjala ser. Esto es América. Nosotros no somos violadores!"* Something about being in America and rape. I was having trouble hearing.

It didn't sound good to me, and I considered my options. They were poor at best. I was in my trunks, waist deep in water, unarmed. Even the element of surprise would be gone before I could cross the sand. I would be a perfect target for a gun, or even a well-thrown knife. They'd simply drag my dead body back out into the Gulf and the sharks would have dessert. That was the way of the sea, nothing going to waste. Ultimate recycling.

I was relieved when I realized they were not following her. They had all opened beers and were toasting something or another.

The sun's light was now completely gone and, without the moon, the water was dark. I stayed low, and the surf covered any noise or movement I made, as I slowly moved south shadowing Angella as she walked carefully back to the tent.

Coming out of the water, I felt a momentary chill as the wind cut across my body. But the night air was warm, and the chill vanished before I intercepted Angella.

"What was all that about?" I asked coming up beside her.

"I was hoping that was you trailing along in the water. Would have been unpleasant if it had been one of them."

"Why didn't you wait for me before you went up there?"

"I thought maybe they'd be more open with a single woman. I know, not the smartest move, but I thought I'd get some intelligence on what they're doing."

"More open? What did you expect a bunch of men to do when a woman shows up in the middle of nowhere? I thought that was why you brought me along."

"Captain wanted me to find out if they had seen anything unusual in the past few nights, such as a boat coming on shore, that type of thing."

"You really think they'd tell you? You guys are smoking something."

"I didn't expect them to try to force me to stay."

"They let you leave. You're lucky."

"The leader let me leave, but the others were angry. They thought they had a live one for the taking. The leader reminded them they were in America."

"I don't understand why you brought me out here if you were going up there alone."

"You're my cover."

"Cover for what? You went alone, how's that cover?"

"They know you're here, that's enough."

"How can you be so sure they know I'm here?"

"They saw you out there fishing. That's why I sent you out. So everyone around will know there's a man here."

"So they cut my throat. I'm a shark's bed-time snack. Why should you care?"

"You read too many cheap detective stories. No one's going to cut anyone's throat."

"Two people already died. If they're involved, you really believe they'll think twice about one more?"

"I'm not sure I follow. One person was found dead on the beach. Another OD'd. They're not tied together. Besides, we don't know for sure the beach incident is tied to anything up here."

"Then why are we here?"

"I'm here because I was told to be here. You're here to give me cover."

"Look, this is not my idea of fun. Let's at least have something to eat. You plan on sitting around the old camp fire singing songs or what?"

"Don't get nasty on me. Dig out the steaks. The coals should be perfect by now. I take it you didn't catch anything."

"You sure know how to pile on when a guy's down."

"Just calling it as it lays."

While I stood guard over the steaks, Angella busied herself with plates and salad. A few sea gulls showed up and began circling. I thought these guys were vegans, but they had their beaks focused on my steak.

When the steaks were ready, I found a beer waiting. Angella was drinking root beer. I suppose she was still in uniform. I guessed there were other activities she didn't participate in while in uniform, but decided to keep my thoughts private, at least for now.

We ate in silence, facing the water and letting the breaking surf carry us away. After a while, I tried a few times to engage her about her visit up the beach, but she continued to deflect. I shifted to her family and got the same treatment. Finally, I said, "I'm beat. Mind if I go off duty."

"Not a problem. In fact, I'll join you as soon as I get this food put away."

"What arrangements do you have in mind?"

"Wrap yourself in a sheet and go to sleep. It's that simple."

"And what about you?"

"I'll do likewise."

"No story telling! That's a bummer."

"You got a story to tell, you tell it."

"None appropriate for the situation."

"And what's the situation?"

"Nothing that you'd understand. I suppose it's a man's thing. Good night, my companion, sweet dreams." I walked up the beach until I could no longer see her, even her silhouette, to relieve myself. I wondered how Angella planned to take care of her bodily needs, but decided that was her problem.

TWELVE

My best guess is that I fell asleep at about midnight. I have no idea when Angella actually fell asleep, but she did just as she said she would, rolled herself up in a sheet like a mummy.

Something brought me awake about an hour later. It couldn't have been a noise, because the surf drowned out all other sounds. Maybe it was the strong sense of presence my sleeping mind sensed. I tried to sit upright, but the sheet prevented me from moving. For an instant, I thought Angella had tied me in, not trusting me to keep away from her. That made no sense. She had the gun.

I began working my arms and hands free and, slowly, the sheet came loose from my body.

At that same instant, a familiar smell made its way past my nose. The smell of urine just beyond the thin fabric of the tent. Then I heard someone stage whisper, "¡Silencio!" a few feet from my head.

I worked the bottom of the tent up a few inches and there was now enough moon light so I could make out four feet moving around in the sand.

"Que uno es el hombre?"

They were trying to determine which one I was. My best guess is that they had not come to ask directions or to find out how the fishing was. The shadow of a machete on the sand moving toward the tent focused my attention.

Angella was wrapped too tightly in her sheet to even get to her gun, assuming I could wake her quickly enough. I had one chance at survival and the only real weapon I possessed was surprise. My guess was that they had other plans for Angella. But then again, Angella dead or alive, may not have been their biggest worry.

I considered working my way out from under the tent and thought better of it. Halfway out and I'd be helpless, my exposed head and neck would make an excellent target. If I could see them then they could see me.

Plan B. Flash a bright light in their eyes and attack them. No light.

Plan C. Call 911.

Plan D. Wait. Wait for them to come into the tent. They'd have to decide which of us to kill first. Since they were concerned about the *hombre* I knew which head would be in the sand first. That meant they'd have to stop and study us for an instant.

Plan E. I was out of plans.

The tent flap moved.

It was the wind.

I heard them whispering, but could make out no words.

I worked my way into a crouch, ready to spring the instant one of them came through the tent opening.

Suddenly, without warning, it happened.

The machete slashed an opening in the tent and the man wielding it filled the opening. He had to crouch to get inside and I wondered why they hadn't cut the tent away to expose both of us. It wasn't as if alarm bells would sound. And even if they did, who would hear them?

The man in the tent swung the machete in front of him and the blade barely missed my face. He was using it for a probe.

It was time to act. The adrenalin surged and I practiced what I had been taught. Count down to action. Three, two, one, go!

I slashed my arm upward as hard as I could, contacting his arm just above the wrist and sending his hand, with the sharp machete in it, upward toward his face.

He had not expected force in that direction and his arm shot upward, the machete tearing through the nylon of the tent and coming to rest against the side of his face. It would have severed his ear except the tent material saved him.

As it was, he let out a scream and, instead of retreating as I had hoped he would, he brought his arm and the lethal weapon back down, slashing into the tent exactly where my arm had hit his.

But as soon I made contact with him I kept driving outward, mindful that I would then become easy prey for his partner. His return slash glanced off my right heel but thankfully the blade had turned slightly and all I felt was a thud as though I had been hit with the shank.

I slammed my right fist into his face and grasped his machete in my left hand, forcing it down against his leg. Another scream filled the air.

Then something hit against my shoulder and, before I could fully turn to see what it was, something else slammed against the side of my head.

I lost my grip on the attacker, and he regained his footing. His arm swung upward to gain momentum for a savage blow. My damaged left arm was not strong enough to prevent the razor edge from severing my neck.

I saw the blade begin its downward arc and I wondered if this was how those condemned to the guillotine spent their last seconds on earth. I tried to move out of the way, but the blow to my head had slowed my reflexes. I was helpless to prevent the blade from cutting straight through me.

The flash came first and lit the beach. The noise that followed was deafening. I fell to the sand.

When I looked up, the two men were backing away, their hands over their heads. Angella's gun was waving between them. Fast Spanish was being exchanged, and I didn't catch a word of it.

After several sharp exchanges, the men turned and ran up the beach and Angella returned to English. "Nice work saving our asses. Sorry to get you into this."

"Why the hell didn't you arrest them?"

"We'll get more from them this way. They're from Mexico. Their friend back at the camp will have their hides. In the morning, we'll get them to tell us what's been going on."

"They'll be long gone by morning."

"Can't, unless they swim home. I have their license number; they can't get off the island."

I started to ask how she got the number and then I remembered her excursion up the beach. *Good work, Angella.*

"In fact, I want them to run. It'll be easier to interrogate them. Up here, I have no jurisdiction. When they pass through SPI we got them." Then she turned her attention on me. "You sure you're okay. Want to go back or stay the night? I'll call this in so they'll be on the lookout for them. Our job's done. This was the group we were hoping to find."

"Why's that?"

"Police business, sorry. So what'll it be? They won't come back, I'll about guarantee that."

"We're here, let's make the most of it."

"Don't be getting any ideas. I still have bullets remaining."

THIRTEEN

Sometime during the night Angella's new found friends from the north must have slipped past us because, when I climbed from the tent about five in the morning, they were gone.

I was relieving myself when Angella called out, "Jimmy, gotta go. Captain says he has a present for me to identify."

"Hope it's more than just one? Should be three?"

"Afraid it's only one. The boss man. The others slipped away somehow."

"Thought you had 'em cornered?"

"You try cornering these people! They're most likely still on the island, only mixed in with the other thousand or so Nationals."

"One guy should be easy to spot. He cut his ear on the machete."

"I'll let them know to be on the look out."

She reached for her radio, and while she was talking, my cell phone let out a beep indicating the arrival of a text message.

The message was from Mark: **Know how body got on beach. Also know who put it there. Think I know why. Off at 0800. See you at Denny's.**

Angella dropped me at my room on her way to the jail. She had refused to give me any more information. In fact, for the last twenty minutes of the ride, she refused to talk at all. I showered and shaved and was on my way to meet Mark when my phone beeped again.

Another message from Mark's cell: **This is Trich Brownsville Hospital. Mark's in a coma. Please come Quick.**

I ran to my car, plugged the hospital name into the GPS, and headed for the bridge. It was going to be at least forty-five minutes before I could get there, so I called my boss.

Before I could get a word in, Contentus barked, "What the hell's going on down there? My phone's ringing off the friggin' hook!"

"Tell me what you've heard, and I'll fill you in on the rest."

"Since when does it work in that direction? Now what the hell do you know? And I want it all!"

He must have read my mind, because I was getting tired of being played with. Either I was in or I was out. Using me for bait is not my idea of a good career move.

I told him about Angella's beach venture and her escapade to the campsite of the Mexican's. I told him about Mark and about my conversation with Joy Malcolm.

Contentus remained silent while I spoke. When I finished, he asked, "That it? Nothing more to add?"

"You think I'm holding back?"

"Just giving you a chance to recall all that's happened down there. You do seem to have a history, if I recall, of not always giving all the facts."

The man never forgot anything. He was referring to a case I had handled six years ago when I did some free-lancing. "That's all from my perspective," I assured him.

"What's Mark have to do with this?" he asked, skepticism apparent in his tone.

"The video we shot while on patrol must be it. He saw something."

"There's no report on file of him being injured. Where did it happen?"

"Don't know?"

"When?"

"I guess sometime after he sent me the text, about five this morning and perhaps six or seven."

"You say his girl friend called you?"

"Text. She used his phone. Must have seen he sent me a text earlier."

"He had to get to the hospital somehow. Being in a coma suggests he didn't drive."

I wanted to say, *you're a Texas Ranger, you figure it out,* but I wanted my job back and politically incorrect talk was not the ticket. "I suppose no one has seen a connection between Mark and the murder, so it's being treated as a routine break-in. From what I can tell down here, they don't have a lot of muggings and physical stuff, so perhaps they thought it was an accident."

"What I don't understand is who the hell called the ambulance? The man's in a coma, he sure as hell didn't take himself to the hospital or call an ambulance. And when was the last time a mugger did that?"

"Maybe he called before he passed out."

"Find out, will you!"

"Without a gun or badge, how the hell you want me to do it?"

"The gun doesn't help investigate. The badge I can't do a thing about. You're on leave and that's that."

I didn't think it prudent to remind him that guns keep investigators alive. "And just why am I here and not someone with an active shield?"

Contentus was silent for longer than I had expected. When he did speak, his voice was low and conspiratorial. "Jimmy, as I told you, we need to keep a low profile a bit longer. DEA is in this up to their hats. Our guy was on loan to them and was on to something. Homeland Security is running a major operation, something to do with terrorists. The two agencies are at each other's throats. That missing file from Mark is a giveaway. Mark found something the brass doesn't like. They want that file. Probably want to bury something."

"So why don't we investigate? That's what we do."

"Governor. Homeland Security leaned on him. He wants this dealt with quietly. Says it's national security and God help us if we get in the way."

"It's always national security when they get their tit in a wringer. What exactly did the Gov'nor say?"

"Not your business. Suffice it to say, he was concerned not to upset the boys in Washington. The man has political ambitions, gotta keep his nose clean."

"And that's where I come in, is what you're saying. I get caught investigating, you deny it. Hang me out. Not much to lose I might add."

"Now don't be bitter. Look at it this way; you're on leave and want back. Do a good job and it might work in your favor."

"Screw up and I'll never see the badge again. That also follows."

"You have such little faith, Jimmy my boy, so little faith."

"I suppose if I said I wanted no more part of this, I'd—"

"Go on permanent leave. You've had a nice career. We'd have one hell of a great party. I might even pay for the beer."

"This the way you treat your friends?"

"Friends? This is business, my lad, business. All's fair. Good luck."

I drove the remainder of the way to the hospital trying to piece it all together.

FOURTEEN

I found a parking spot in the hospital parking lot and sent a text to Mark's phone telling Trich where I was.

She immediately responded: **Use front door. Take elevator to 4ᵗʰ. I'll have a pen in my right hand.**

The elevator door opened and, from the devastated look on her face, I didn't have to bother checking for a pen.

"I'm Jimmy," I said and threw my arms around her.

Her body shook while I held her. Gradually, she regained her composure. "He's in the OR. They had to drill into his skull to relieve the pressure. Won't know anything for a while. I'm off duty. Can't do a thing anyway."

"What happened?" I asked, trying to not sound very official. "Is there a place where we can talk in private?"

She led me around a corner to an alcove with several tables and chairs. "Don't know for sure," she replied when we both were seated. "Anonymous caller to the South Padre Police. Caller said a man had fallen. He gave the address and told the dispatcher the man needed helicopter evac." When the police arrived, he was laying on his back. Fire rescue stabilized him and brought him here."

"How did you know he was here?"

"This is a small place. When the rescue crew called it in, a friend of mine immediately called me. He looked awful. I didn't think he'd make it. He still might not."

"I'm sorry," I replied lamely. Trich's grieving eyes told the whole story. She was a beautiful woman, not as tall as I had imagined, but elegant, with a classically beautiful face. She had tight, clear skin and pronounced cheekbones. Her grieving carried into her voice and made her sound tentative, unsure of her words. "We were so happy together. He's the best person I've ever known. He told me you know about us getting married."

I nodded and she continued, "Did he tell you he wanted you as his best man?"

That caught me completely by surprise. Now I was unsure of my voice. "No," I managed. "He told me about you and how he didn't know how to tell his mother. But he didn't mention anything about best man."

"He didn't know how to ask. He's a person of extraordinary inner strength, but under it all, he has trouble when people mean a lot to him. You, his mother, sometimes even me. He wants to be perfect and is always afraid of not living up."

"I know about his wanting to be perfect, but I never knew he was afraid to fail. He hides it well."

"Yes, he does. Speaking of his mother, can you please call her? It would be strange coming from me."

That was not a task I relished, but it was a necessary one. Calling a parent after a child had been injured, or worse killed, was for me the worst part of being in law enforcement.

I called the airline, booked a flight, called my former partner Lonnie Turner, and explained the situation to him. He agreed to pick up Mark's mother in an hour. Then I called Nora Cruses.

"Oh, my baby," she kept repeating over and over. "My poor baby."

She wanted me to assure her he would live, but all I could manage was, "He's in good hands." A very unsettling message at best, but I was never good at candy coating these types of things. After she calmed down, I told her to be ready in an hour, that Lonnie was coming for her. She knew Lonnie from her husband's retirement party. We were all so young then, so innocent. The world hadn't beaten on us. Even my shoulder functioned well back then.

When I hung up, I turned to Trich. "I didn't tell her about you. There's time enough when she gets here. It'll be about one, maybe one-thirty before I get back from the airport with her. Hope we have some good news by then."

"My guess is that they won't know much for at least twenty-four hours. I've seen all too many head traumas, and they don't often end well."

"Let's hope for the best. Is there a chapel in the hospital?"

"Yes," She answered, terror filled her eyes. "Do you know something—"

"Then let's go and say a prayer for him."

"He told me you were Catholic, but that you don't go much anymore."

"Off and on."

"He went every Sunday when he was off duty. I loved to go and sit next to him. He prayed with the same intensity that he did everything else. Being beside him, feeling his warmth, gave me a strength I didn't know I had."

"I wouldn't have expected anything other than that from him."
We walked to the chapel, my arm around her to steady her.

After we left the chapel, I said, "While we're waiting, mind if I
get something to eat? I missed breakfast."

"I'd join you but the smell of food won't sit well with me. I
couldn't eat a thing. I'll wait for you up in his room."

I was eating a bowl of oatmeal and sipping lukewarm coffee
when a small compact bulldog of a man slipped into the chair across
the table from me. "You're Jimmy Redstone, friend of Lieutenant
Markus Joseph Cruses," he said, without preamble. "I'm his commanding officer, Captain Ernest Boyle."

I began to extend my hand in greeting but thought better of
it when I realized he had no intention of being sociable. Instead, I
replied, "So to what do I owe this honor?"

"What the hell were you doing on the patrol boat?" he
barked.

"Mark invited me." This man was bad news and the less information I gave him the better.

"That's against regulations!"

"I have no knowledge of that fact," I answered, holding my
ground.

"I'm saying you were trespassing on government property! You
have a smart-ass answer for that?"

"I repeat what I already said. I know nothing of Coast Guard
rules or regulations. If I did something improper I did so inadvert-
ently." He had no jurisdiction over a civilian not now on government
property, so I decided to call his bluff. "You think I did something
wrong, take it up with the police. I have nothing more to say on this
subject. Now, unless you have something to discuss with me in a
civil tone, kindly move away from my table and allow me to finish
breakfast."

His face hardened even more and a large artery bulged along the side of his neck. "Lieutenant Cruses will answer for this! He's had a fine record to this point, but he's off the reservation on this one."

"I'm truly sorry to hear that. You might have to wait a while to reprimand him, however. Seems he *fell* this morning and hit his head. Not looking good."

"Lieutenant Cruses accident is certainly a shame, but not your concern."

I studied him for a moment, and then summoning my most condescending voice, said, "When I was in the service, commanding officers showed a bit more concern for the well-being of their charges. Times certainly have changed. You have no call to tell me who I should care about. Mark's well-being is most definitely my concern. He's a long-time friend and I have every right to be here for him."

"Don't go lecturing me on how to do my job! Man violates rules, man gets punished. That's the way it's always worked and that's the way it works now. Do you understand?"

"He's near death and you're worried about a rule he broke, if he broke a rule at all. Now say what you came to say and get away from here. I'm trying to eat."

His hands balled into fists and he clenched and unclenched them several times. His neck was so red I thought the artery was about to burst.

He stood, his feet apart as I would expect from a man who spends considerable time at sea, and grasped the chair in front of him. "Just stay the hell out of Coast Guard business, you understand me?"

"I'm not involved in Coast Guard business, so no, I don't understand. You care to elaborate?"

"You come across Coast Guard files Lieutenant Cruses had, you call me immediately, you understand." He fumbled in his coat pocket for a card and slammed it on the table hard enough to cause cream to splash from the pitcher.

"And just how would I even recognize a Coast Guard file?" I asked, playing dumb to get information and not give away the fact that I already knew what he was talking about.

"Videos taken from the craft you were on for one thing."

"How in the world would I have anything such as that?"

He studied me for a long moment, the blood moving upward from his neck and causing his face to flush. "For one thing, your young friend seems to have an unauthorized copy of a highly confidential video taken from one or more patrol craft. I have reason to think you have it, or at least know where it is."

"Let me assure you I do not have such a file."

"And let me assure you that your life will be most unpleasant if you don't turn those files over to me."

I jumped to my feet and started around the table. I tried to mask the fact that my left arm drooped, but Boyle's eyes locked on my left side. He held his ground. I shoved my face as close to his as I could and, in a voice low enough so only he could hear, I said, "You threaten me again and we'll see which one of us walks away. For now, I'll honor the uniform and not kick your ass from here to Sunday. You have no authority over civilians. None whatsoever, so you better watch how you talk. You wear that uniform, you're supposed to act like a gentleman. You better go back and learn that part of your training. Now get the hell away from me before they have to rebuild your ugly face."

We stood that way for a while, neither of us giving an inch. I was ready for him, but determined he would have to throw the first blow.

Boyle's military training finally took hold. He eased his stance and stepped back. "The next time we meet," he snarled, "I can assure you, you won't be so cocky. See how you like life in the brig. You ever hear of the term enemy combatant and Guantanamo? You're messing with Coast Guard operations, be warned." With that he turned and walked away.

Something important must be going down when the commanding officer of a dying man is more interested in a video than in the man who has the video.

To me, that meant a few things, none of which I liked. For starters, he knew Mark didn't have the video, at least not anymore. I wondered if he was responsible in some way for the accident. Second, the dead guy on the beach, and perhaps the OD guy, were only an annoyance to him. The real show hadn't yet taken center stage.

FIFTEEN

When I arrived back at Mark's room, Trich told me he was in recovery and the doctors were guardedly hopeful. When I pressed her on what that meant, she wiped away a tear and said, "That's doctor speak for *anything can happen*. From my experience, this can go either way. They'll keep him in a coma for at least a day and maybe two and then bring him out slowly. The preliminary tests indicate everything seems to be responding within the normal range."

On a hunch, I asked, "Do you still have his cell phone, the one you sent the text from?"

"Sure I do."

"Mind if I see it?"

She pulled out her bag, fumbled among its contents, shook her head several times and finally said, "It seems to be missing. I know it's here. I had it a while ago." She proceeded to empty her purse and the only cell phone on the table was hers.

"When did you see it last?"

"I know I put it in my purse right after I used it to text you." She thought for a moment, and then added, "Sure I did. You sent me a text when you got here. I had it then."

"Was the purse out of your sight at all?"

She paused again. "I went to the restroom while you were eating. I think I left my bag in Mark's room. But I was only gone a minute or two. I can't imagine anyone getting into it that fast."

Either the Captain, or someone who worked for him, took it. "Did you see anyone in the hall outside his room?"

"No one special, but there was a man walking down the hall when I came out of the restroom."

"Try to recall what he looked like. It may be important later on."

"What's this about? Is Mark into something?"

"Don't really know. But he might not have fallen, that's all I can say at this point. Give me you cell number so I can get in touch with you." She gave me her number and I copied it directly into my phone. I wrote my cell number on a card and handed it to her. "Don't forget to call if anything comes up. Anything at all."

"I need him. I hope he'll be okay. I don't know what I'll do without him. He's my life."

"All we can do is pray for him. What the doctor said I'll take as good news." I turned to leave and changed my mind. "I'm going to the airport to get his mother. Want to come along and meet Mom, or would you prefer to stay here?"

"I'll go. Hospitals don't foster good thoughts."

The Brownsville airport proved to be a relatively tiny place and reminiscent of a time in America long past. We had plenty of time to kill and, after pacing back and forth across the length of the small terminal several times, we decided to walk around the parking area. Twice around the small lot took almost no time so we extended our hike several blocks into an industrial zone. We talked about Mark, and I filled Trich in on what little I knew of Mark's mother Nora.

From my observation, Nora was a quiet woman, who kept a neat house and spent her life taking care of Mark, Sr., and Jr. She referred to her husband and her son as her boys and she doted on both.

She was always proud of her son, showing his picture to anyone who would look. He had played running back in high school and she never missed a game. I don't think she even knew what the object was, but if Mark had the ball you could hear her voice above the crowd.

I spoke to Trich about how Mark had lettered all four years but refused a scholarship to several major universities, including the University of Texas and A&M. Instead, he went to New London, Connecticut, to attend the Coast Guard Academy. It was a tough decision between there and the Navy at Annapolis, but he opted for the smaller school, even though Navy had offered him a football scholarship.

Not surprising, Mark had told Trich none of this. He had always been one who let his actions speak for him, so the fact that he was the team captain for both his junior and senior years was unknown to his fiancé.

We were talking about trust in relationships, and suddenly her mood changed from jovial to serious, very serious. Obviously making a decision, she said, "There's something important I need to tell you. Something I should have told Mark long ago but was afraid to."

We stopped walking and I turned to her. "You sure you should tell me before you tell Mark?"

"It's important. You can help."

Before she could say anything further, a plane came in low directly over us. I instinctively glanced at my watch and realized that

Nora was on that plane. "I hate to interrupt your thoughts, but we can only get back to the terminal in time if we jog back. I'm sorry, I lost track of time."

"That's okay. We'll pick this up later." We turned and began to jog. In less than a block I had to slow down. The one-hundred-degree temperature, along with the humidity, had already sapped me.

It was then that I realized we had a tail. Professional, judging from the fact that I had not noticed anything until we unexpectedly began to run, and then suddenly stopped.

I said to Trich, "Don't stare. Make your head motions look natural, but I need you to observe the man across the street. By any chance is that the guy you saw in the hospital?"

We went another half-block before she answered. "It could be, looks to have the same build, but I'm not positive. He's keeping his head averted."

"Okay. Just ignore him. We'll deal with that later. Mom's waiting for us."

Sweat poured from me when I entered the terminal and the cool air felt arctic on my over-heated body. I frantically ran my eyes around the lobby, hopping to spot a water fountain. Instead, I saw Nora hurrying down the hallway, a large purse swinging from her shoulder.

"Jimmy," she exclaimed, when we came across the lobby toward her, "I thought you forgot. How is he? How's my boy? My you look a fright. Like you're about to burst a blood vessel, or something. You're so red. Better sit down."

"I'll be fine," I managed. "It's mighty hot out there. This air conditioning will cool me down quick." Trich had held back to give me time to talk with Nora privately.

I sugar coated the news a bit, giving her more hope than I felt at the moment, being careful to add, "The doctors really don't know anything for sure yet. It'll be another day." I explained about the coma and added, "It'll be important to have you there to talk to him. Sometimes they understand, even if they can't respond."

She asked several questions and hugged me over and over. "Oh, Jimmy, he's all I have left. I need him to be well."

"I know, Nora, we all need him." I looked toward Trich and motioned her to come forward. When she did, I said, "Nora, we have some good news for you. A surprise Mark was saving for you. He's engaged to be married and this is his fiancé." I introduced Trich by her full name of Patricia May Rodriguez Santiago. "Her friends call her Trich."

"Oh, my! Is this why Mark hasn't been to visit me? Not like him at all to forget his mother. Too busy now that he has someone he likes, I suppose." She studied Trich and then held out her hand, "It is indeed a pleasure meeting you. I hate to spoil Mark's surprise, but considering the circumstances, it's better we meet now than wait for him to get better. I'm sure Mark selected well. He always does everything well. He is such a good boy. Always was a good boy. He's all I have, you know."

"I know, Mrs. Cruses," Trich responded. "Mark speaks so much about you. It seems I already know you."

"You have an accent. Is that from Mexico?"

"Yes," Trich answered. "I am Mexican." She pulled back a step and stood in silence, her lips curling downward ever so slightly, while she waited for Nora to respond. The rigidity in her body gave away her apprehension.

"Oh, I know he has chosen well," Nora said, stepping close to Trich and pulling the slender woman close enough to hug. "You do know, I hope, Mark's great-grandfather came from Mexico. That was a long time ago. You'll be right at home in our family. I know you'll make Mark very happy. He's a good boy."

Mark was still not back in his room when we returned to the hospital, and so I checked Nora into a motel a block away. Trich said she'd look after her future mother-in-law, the two of them planning on catching an early dinner and then waiting in Mark's room until he was brought back.

Trich promised to call me as soon as she heard anything. I took that as my dismissal and headed back to the island for some much needed rest.

SIXTEEN

Indeed, I did get a good night's sleep, waking at nine the next morning. I hadn't slept past six for months, and I was momentarily upset that I had missed my trainer appointment. The thought of having a leisurely breakfast quickly dissipated my regrets. One day, more or less, wouldn't make a bit of difference.

I checked my cell phone to be sure I hadn't missed a message from Trich. Nothing there, so I headed out to *Ted's* and ordered a stack of pecan pancakes and washed them down with two cups of coffee. That did the trick. I was ready to face the day.

I walked out of *Ted's* and the high cloudless sky caused me to squint while I fished out my sunglasses. I stepped aside to make way for an attractive woman, her lower right leg in a black walking boot. The brave soul was butt-walking up the concrete steps, determined to have breakfast in the small restaurant that I understood was an institution on the Island for more years than most can remember.

Her escort, a bald, bearded man, bent to help her to her feet when she reached the landing. I commented, "You must really like this place to go to all that trouble."

Without hesitation she flashed a knowing smile. "Been coming here for over ten years. Need my pecan pancake fix. No place else makes them like *Ted's*. Even my son and daughter-in-law from Paris love to come here."

"This was my first time," I responded, "and I agree. They were excellent. I can understand why the French enjoy it. Enjoy your day."

Her smile widened. "On South Padre Island, what's there not to enjoy? Even in a wheel chair you can't beat it here."

My cell announced the presence of a new text message. I climbed into my car, left the door open for a moment, started the engine to chase away the heat, and flipped the phone open to read the message: **Mark back in his room. Still in Coma. Will be in coma another day. Doc says if he continues this progress he'll fully recover. More later.**

Good news. Instead of heading directly to the hospital, I decided to drive north and do a bit of sightseeing while the pancakes were digesting. Then I'd change and head to the gym and back to the routine.

Within about two miles, the housing construction was all behind me, and all I could see was sand and more sand on both sides of the road. The terrain was flat, but large sand dunes had formed on both sides of the road. The comparison of the view with what I imagined a lunar landscape to be was inescapable. I visualized men in helmets and spacesuits coming over a ridge.

Suddenly, the cold imprint of steel against the back of my neck shocked me back to reality. A hand reached past my face and slammed the rear-view mirror down.

"Don't turn around!" a voice barked, directly behind me, only inches from my ear. "It won't take much for me to pull the trigger! Keep driving."

I glanced at the outside mirrors but they were useless to see who was behind me. I concentrated on replaying his speech pattern in my head and realized it was vaguely familiar.

"What do you want from me?" I asked, trying to get him talking. "If it's money, I don't have much, but you can have it all. It's in my wallet."

"Its not money, asshole!" The gun pushed further into my neck, and my fingers tingled from the pressure. "You have a video file. I want that file!"

"I don't have any files."

"Don't screw with me! It's on a disk of some kind. You got it. I want it!"

"I don't have what you want. You can search me, but I have nothing you want."

"I plan to do just that, asshole. If you're lying I'll shoot your sorry ass!"

"You won't find it 'cause I don't have it."

"Listen carefully! One false move and you're dead. Understand?"

"Understand." I answered. From the tone of his voice I was convinced he was serious.

"Slow down," he commanded. "Up ahead, there's an opening in the dunes on the left. Stay on the hard sand or this shit heap will get stuck. That'll be the end of you if that happens. Pull off into the opening. There it is! See it?"

"Yes."

"Turn in and follow the packed sand. Slow way down!"

I did as he instructed, and the car fishtailed as it came off the paved road. The gun pressed even harder.

The car settled down, and I struggled to follow the hard packed area, which was barely wider than the wheelbase. It was rutted with deep crevices and the car bottomed out several times.

Then everything went dark.

A canvas bag had been pulled over my head and a drawstring, or rope, held it tight around my neck.

"What the hell!" I shouted, "Can't see to drive!"

"Hit the brake asshole! Get your ass out of the car and lay on the ground. You remove that bag, you're a dead man! You make one move to get up, you're a dead man!"

I found the door handle, opened it and took two steps.

"Get your ass down!" he shouted. "One last chance. You have that file, you give it to me, you go home a free man. I have to find it and you're dead. Now do you have it?"

"No."

"Pull everything from your pockets. Let it spill on the sand. And I mean everything!"

I did as I was instructed.

"That everything?"

"Yes."

"Pull your pockets inside out!"

He then patted me down, not missing a spot.

"Take off your shirt and pants!"

"What the hell?"

"Do it! You're in no position to negotiate anything. Everything off!" He waited while I pulled my shorts and underwear off. "Now stand! Spread your legs!"

One thing I now knew for certain. This guy was a drug dealer. He was accustomed to people hiding things in their body orifices. He was looking for a telltale string hanging out, or some other telltale sign.

"Pull your butt apart! Wider! Wider!"

Then he shoved me back onto the sand.

"Don't move while I search your car."

I couldn't see what he was doing, but judging from the sounds I heard, he examined every possible crack and crevice. I knew he had to have put the gun down to work, but I had no idea of exactly where he was and, without being able to see, I had no hope of getting to him before he got to his gun. I didn't know the landscape so I couldn't make a break for it.

My best chance to get out of this alive was to do nothing. Not an option I liked, but the only one currently available. Even then it was doubtful I wouldn't be shot.

I tried to focus on why he hadn't shot me right off, and all I could think of was he might need me to show him how the file worked if he found it. Since I didn't have the file, that ace was not going to work.

Eventually, I heard his footsteps coming closer. I braced to grab his leg and throw him over as I had been trained to do back in my Army Ranger days. It had all seemed so easy then. A few well-placed moves and you win. That may have worked when I was twenty, but thirty years later, it all seemed so very far away—and impossible.

"You thinking of grabbing my leg, forget it, asshole! You just stay where you are and you'll be fine. Like you said, you don't seem to have what I'm looking for, so I have no grudge with you. Don't give me a reason to shoot you now. Fifteen minutes, you're free to go. You lay there fifteen minutes, then do what the hell you want. I'll be long gone. To show you I have no grudge, I even left your cell phone. It's in the car. One catch. The car's locked so don't try making a break for it. You're not going anywhere for a while. I'll drop the keys out by the road. Remember, fifteen minutes and then you're free to go find the keys."

And then there was silence.

I started a mental timer, knowing full well there was no point in cutting it short. I wasn't going to find this guy, even if I only counted to one hundred. All I was likely to do was get shot. This was his territory, not mine. My best bet was to lick my wounds and preserve myself to fight another day. That's not what I would have done twenty years ago, but it had to suffice now.

SEVENTEEN

It took me over two hours to find my keys, put my car back together as best I could, and head back to the TIKI. All thoughts of going to the gym were gone. One thing for certain, working without a partner was not high on my priority list.

I had tried several times to call Contentus and could not get through to his cell. I tried the main number, and the dispatcher, a man I knew well, simply said he was in the field and would return my call. He refused to tell me when that would be.

I opened the door to my room and, before the door was fully open, I knew at least one person was in the room. "Shit!" I exclaimed to myself, "here we go again!" This time I was determined to not be passive.

I ducked and rolled to the left in the direction the door had swung, reaching for my non-existent gun in the process. The maneuver was useless without a weapon, and I felt foolish.

"You mind telling me what the hell you're doing Redstone?" the familiar voice asked, "After explaining why you're on the floor, you can tell me what kind of mess you've gotten yourself into now."

I was angry and my shoulder throbbed from being bounced against the concrete floor. But above all, I felt foolish. I certainly wasn't in the mood for pleasantries, even though it was my boss who was sitting on the sofa, his lips curled into a wry smile. "You mind telling me what the hell you're doing in my room scaring me half to death?"

"First, get your sorry ass off the floor! Case you haven't heard, Redstone, you're way beyond that barrel roll shit! You're lucky I didn't put a bullet though your head while you were still in the air!"

I pulled myself up, using the door for support. I certainly wasn't twenty any longer, and any residual doubt I might have had was now wiped away.

When I was seated, Contentus said, "I suppose I do owe that to you. Good thing you're not armed or this coulda been messy. I might have ended up like Badman Tex. But truth to tell, in the process, I would have taken out your other shoulder." He smiled for one of the rare times in our relationship. "You been messing with the Coast Guard. What the hell's that about?"

"I'd say they were messing with me! Captain Boyle, Mark Cruses' commander, accosted me in the hospital cafeteria. Seems to think I have some videos taken when I was out with Mark. I'm convinced Mark was attacked by Boyle's men."

"You know that as a fact or as a supposition?"

"Supposition. Ostensibly he fell at his apartment and hit his head. He's in a coma for at least another day."

"You think Mark's accident is not a slip and fall?"

"I've been trying to reach you for the past two hours." I went on to tell him about my encounter on the sand dunes. "I can't believe this guy was one of ours. He's a drug trade professional if ever there was one."

"Why professional?"

"Knew how to handle himself. Got what he wanted without an unnecessary dead body bringing in more cops. A simple thug would have taken the easy way out. This was well planned and executed. Didn't use a gang to do it. Man has self-confidence."

"So you think it was the Coast Guard? Makes no sense."

"Mark saw something on that video, something a lot of people want. Judging from the good Captain and what he said to me, I know the Coast Guard wants it for sure." I dug out my cell and brought up the text message from Mark. **Know how body got on beach. Also know who brought it in. Think I know why. Off at 0800. See you at Denny's.**

"Someone lifted Mark's cell from Trich, that's his fiancé, at the hospital. My guess, it was the work of the Coast Guard. That's why Boyle's on to me. So, why you here? The phone works."

"Save the resentment. This is not all bad news for you. You've been restored to active status, at least for the duration of this assignment. That could be good or bad, I won't try to guess that one." He fumbled in his well-worn shoulder bag and brought out my badge. A bit more rummaging and my Beretta appeared along with a box of cartridges. "Here, you just might be needing these."

I didn't ask how he came by my gun. Some things are best left with the imagination. I also didn't ask how he managed to get me certified as fit for duty. "I thought we weren't getting involved," I said, probing for more information, even while knowing Contentus never passed out more than was necessary. He wrote the book on *need to know*.

"Simple. A Texas Ranger was murdered! The Governor fields a call asking for the Rangers to stay out of the fray. What the hell you think I'm going to do, forget it!"

"What did you tell the Governor?"

"A Ranger dies, we're involved. It's just that simple. Governor backed down, said he was just passing along what he had been asked to pass along. Wished me luck at finding the killer." Contentus glanced out of the window before continuing, "That's where you come in. On the surface, it appears we honored their request. We're not bringing in the cavalry. Captain Boyle, or whoever is behind this, doesn't yet know you're with us, so we can play that for a while, see where it goes."

"Does the SPI Chief know who I am?"

"Yes. I couldn't allow you to work here, on or off the record, without his permission. He's a good guy, and we've had a good working relationship over the years."

"That means when Angella, Officer Martinez, asked him to let me join her on that beach fiasco, he knew what was going on."

"He knew she had met you and made it look like it was her idea. The man knows what the hell's going on down here. It was also coordinated with the County police. That group she approached, that was not a random act on her part. She was instructed to go up there and prod them a bit. The County folks have had an eye on them for a while. They're regulars on the beach up there, almost always at the same location. The night Nelson, that's our guy who got his neck cut, was found, a shipment of cocaine arrived by boat and was dropped just off the beach. County believes those three guys, maybe with some help, brought it in. What we don't know is why they're still out there. Usually, they lay low for a month or so after a drop. That's what's bothering the boys down here."

"But they left in the middle of the night. SPI got the top banana, I understand the other two got away."

"Couldn't hold him. He's back on the street—or in this case— on the sand. The other two were dropped before he came off the beach. The guy you cut hasn't turned up, but he will. He left a lot of blood in the sand. Actually, we know who he is. Name's Paco Santino. That's his handle so to speak. Real name's Billy Jaspers. Guy's been in the drug trade since birth. His father, William, was a top dog in the Gulf Cartel, until he was killed in a shoot out with a Mexican gang. Actually, Paco's the leader. The guy they got is a low-life who Paco uses to front the operation. They've taken to calling them *se enfrenta a falsos*. For short, *falsos*. Loosely, phony faces. Some retrograde gets to parade around pretending to be the boss man. When the shooting starts, he's the first to fall."

"So where's this guy Paco? How did he slip through?"

"He didn't, as far as we know. He's on the island and getting medical treatment. Someone needs him here. Something else is coming in."

"What else do you have? Seems you've been a busy beaver."

"Not me, I just monitor what's going on. The SPI and the County folks are running this one. Oh, one other thing. Nelson's head was severed with a wire of some kind. Man was garroted!"

"Why is that important?" I asked, not yet putting it all together.

"We think maybe a ritual of some sort."

"Maybe a monofilament fishing line from a shrimp boat," I offered, recoiling at the visual image.

"Could be, but our best guess is that Nelson was tagged as a Ranger, or maybe just an unspecified lawman, his neck cut, the body thrown overboard, washed up on the beach."

"Then why call the Coast Guard? That's why Mark and I went out in the first place."

"Someone else did. But that's what has us puzzled."

"So what's my role in this? You're not here to simply talk. Could have done that on the phone. You're here to sell me on something. How about letting me in on it."

"Maybe I just love the beach."

"Your wife would be with you, not me."

"I came to bring you your weapon and to visit personally with the Chief."

"And?"

"And to ask you to work with Officer Martinez, but to do so as you did before, undercover."

"Is she to know?"

"She's being briefed by the Chief as we speak."

"So you assumed I'd go along and partner with an untrained rookie. That's suicide in a mission like this and you know it."

"She's not exactly a rookie, but yes, she's not trained as a Ranger. That bother you?"

"Of course it bothers me! How the hell will she cover my back if I have to tell her what to do every step of the way."

"Chief claims she's a quick learner. Anyway, the operation is beyond that now. It's sink or swim. I suggest you swim."

"So that's who you've been expecting, Martinez?"

"You haven't lost your sharpness I see. That's good, 'cause you're going to need everything you can throw at this."

"What's that supposed to mean?"

"Nothing you haven't already worked out. Something big's going down—and going down soon. When the United States Armed Forces get involved, one dead guy on the beach, or to be blunt, a dead Ranger, is simply collateral damage."

EIGHTEEN

It's amazing how putting the badge back in my hands cleared my head. Actually, the cavity search on the sand dunes had triggered a thought. As soon as the boss walked out, I called Trich. "How long does it take an object to pass through the digestive system?" I asked when she came on the line.

"Don't know, why?"

"I think Mark swallowed the file. Is he still in the room?"

"Yes. His mother's with him. She and I had a nice long talk. I think we'll get along fine. She alternates between hugging me and crying. Now she's hugging Mark and holding his hand. If love can bring him back, then he'll make it."

"He's tough, he'll make it. Listen, I want you to check his diaper, or whatever in the hell he's wearing, for the drive. If I'm right, he'll pass it soon."

"It's going to be hard to do. The nurse's aide does that and I can't just go in and undress him."

"It's important. You're a nurse; nobody's going to pay any mind to you cleaning him up. You two are engaged, it's the least you can do."

"I don't know if I can do it."

"Why not?"

The line went dead. I thought I had lost her. Then, softly, she responded, "We need to talk."

"We'll talk when I get there. For now, check him."

"I'll do what I can."

"It's important. We need that file."

"I'll try."

I hung up and called Angella. Before she could say anything, I said, "Run a name for me. See what comes up. She's a nurse at Brownsville Hospital." I gave her Trich's name and added, "It's a rush. Could save a good man's life."

The line went silent for a few minutes and, when Angella came back, she said, "It'll take a while. They're running lots of names."

"Should I call Austin? How long will it take here?"

"Maybe an hour."

"Okay, you coming over here or what?"

"Whatever you want. Apparently, I'm at your service. Chief told me to cooperate, so I'm cooperating."

"So what's the problem? You sound miffed."

"Wouldn't you be? At least you could have told me you were a Ranger. Decorated at that. Never heard the Chief say a nice word about anyone. You he can't say enough about. I feel the fool."

"Orders are orders. I was told to lay low. Just doing my job. So were you. Comes with the territory. You have to get used to it. Did the Chief give you any direction to take?"

"Said you'd do what you wanted anyway, so I may as well go with the flow. Told me to take my lead from you. I'm assigned to you full time. Your call. I'll grease the skids so to speak. He told me no uniform. You agree?"

Well, at least I got her out of uniform. I reminded myself to be careful how I phrased my wishes. "I agree. We need to remain below the radar as much as is possible." I thought about what I knew so far and it wasn't much. I had a few people I could run down, but nothing that screamed for attention. "Who can brief me on all that's gone down so far?"

"Chief. He's running this personally."

"When can we get with him?"

"Say, fifteen minutes. He said you'd ask for a briefing first thing. Come on over so he's not disappointed. City Hall, the *new* City Hall, room 210. He's set up over there."

I put Chief Duran at about age fifty-eight. A well-built man who, judging from the strength of his grip and the stretching of his shirt across his chest, kept himself in good shape. Probably worked out at the gym. His smile quickly faded, and he got right to business.

"You come to us highly regarded and a bit damaged," he snapped. "I welcome you here, and I hope you're physically up to it."

I glanced down at my shoulder.

"No, not your shoulder, I mean your mental conditioning. Teran already told me you were in good physical shape." He held his hand up to stop my protest. "I'm not here to debate mental health with you, only to get assurance you understand you're working for me on this investigation and not Contentus. And certainly not for yourself. You can report anything you wish to him, but I want assurance you're on our team and anything and everything you find comes to me first. God help you, if I find you leaking stuff to him before I get it! Do I make myself clear enough?"

I nodded, and he snapped, "I want to hear it from your lips. You Rangers think you're above it all. I won't be having any of that shit!"

"I understand I'm working for you on this investigation. I'll report what I find directly to you before it goes to headquarters. That what you want to hear?"

"I'll overlook the tone of that, but you better understand up front I don't book bullshit. Understood?"

"Understood," I replied, trying to determine how much of this was bluff and how much real.

"Okay, now we understand each other. I'm a hands on guy. You'll be working with Angella, and I know what you think of working with rookies. I also know you think you saved her ass up on the beach last night, but they weren't coming for her. They wanted you."

How the hell would he know that? I wondered.

"Don't look so puzzled. They knew you were in the water when Angella got into it with them. These guys are professionals. They won't underestimate you again, and don't for a moment think they're fools. Paco, the guy you cut, is a mean son of a bitch. He would just as soon cut your throat as say hello. A real gem. We knew he was up there and wanted to flush him, to disrupt their operation, their timing. I thought something might be coming in last night, and I wanted him edgy."

"Why?"

"I'm getting there. Guy that was killed on the beach, as you know, was a Ranger working undercover for the Drug Enforcement folks. He had infiltrated the Southwest drug group. DEA believes they must have realized he was not one of them and threw him overboard. That means he was with them when they were delivering the drugs, and they discovered he was a plant or they would have cut his throat and left him to rot in Mexico. Maybe he was using his cell or a radio to coordinate a bust, I don't know. The DEA isn't as forthcoming as one would like."

Duran went to the door and closed it. He returned to his seat behind a table cluttered with files and binders. "Coast Guard's mixed up in this, as you already know. That puts Homeland Security directly against DEA. We're caught in the middle. Have a murder, actually two, to clear, and they're not cooperating. What bothers me is where your friend Cruses fits into this. Nice boy. Runs a good base here on the Island. He and I have a good working relationship. His men stay out of trouble for the most part. A little too much drinking from time to time, but show me a service person doesn't wet his whistle on his time off, and I'll show you a real dud."

"Something's going down then," I ventured. "I mean whatever this is, Mark knows more than he should and his boss is worried. Coast Guard can't be running drugs, I'd have heard something."

"We all would. No, they're not in the drug trade, but they're doing something that doesn't feel right. The second death, the guy who OD'd, was most likely murdered. He was a low life from San Antone and did drugs from time to time, but was never busted before this. Most likely was not a big user. Died of an overdose. Looks to be forced on him."

"That's consistent with what Joy Malcolm told me," I confirmed.

He pounded his fist on the table. "This is what I'm talking about! Your boss had you snooping down here, and I'm not in the loop! But I need to get the information direct, not this round about cat and mouse bullshit! Now, what the hell else you holding back?"

Now it was my turn to assert myself. "Chief, I told you I was playing on your team. I meant it. I'm here to serve you and work with you, but I'm a Ranger first, last, and always, and I don't take shit from anybody. There's no need to threaten me. I'll give you what you want. But you're off base here. I was just having lunch with the woman and she told me about him. In fact, she told the whole bar the other night. She sought me out, not vice versa."

Instead of confronting me, Chief Duran ignored my rant and went on. "Tell me how you came to have lunch with Mrs. Joy Malcolm."

"I was having a late snack with Angella and, when Angella left, Malcolm sought me out. Had a few too many and got into it with me and her husband. Bumped into her the next day at the gym and she invited me to lunch. Told me about cheating on her husband with Heart. That's when she said Heart's death was not accidental." A troubling thought flittered in and out of my consciousness. Something to do with Heart.

"How'd she track you down?"

"Saw me at the gym. Lady cleans up nice, have to say that for her. I didn't know she was married, thought the man she was with was a bit old for her, but was mistaken." As I spoke, the thought took hold and I debated whether to share it with the Chief or run it to ground myself. I decided to share. "Something's troubling me. You said Heart was a low life. Joy clearly told me he was a teacher, a high school coach I recall she said. Hardly a low life."

"For a man just out having lunch you sure get information. That's right. Joy told us the same story. Only it's not accurate. By the way, thanks for playing on the team and not withholding. We have reason to believe Joy knew exactly who he was. Her husband is someone we need to get more intelligence on. Seems a quiet man, no record we can find. Joy gets drunk; he takes her home. No yelling, nothing of that sort. Seems devoted to her. No sign of gainful employment, but that doesn't stop him from spending it."

"Malcolm says she supports him and is tired of it. Gambles."

"Gambling seems to be a cover as far as we can tell. Nothing big that is. Man's a mystery and I don't believe in mysteries, especially not when a wife's lover is found dead. You two work that for a while."

"Has Angella ever worked investigations?"

"A virgin." He cracked a slight smile, "In that department, anyway. Husband left her not long ago, don't know why. Every man on the department has made a run at her one time or another. To my knowledge all to no avail. Maybe she goes the other way."

"Hope we're not being recorded."

"Just stating a fact is all. Don't underestimate her. She's one tough lady and about the best shooter on the force. She follows orders. She's got street smarts and gets the job done. Got a great future. Don't ruin it."

I didn't have to ask who the best shooter on the force was. I already knew that answer.

- - - -

"There's no nurse at Brownsville name of Patricia May Rodriguez Santiago," Angella reported when I left the Chief. She had changed out of her uniform and was wearing shorts and a loose-fitting blouse that still revealed an ample figure. I could see why men would make a run at her. Now that she was my partner a crimp had been put in my desire to make a run of my own.

"There's got to be," I replied, forcing myself back to business. The last time I had had a female partner, we got sexually tangled, and it didn't end well. I didn't intend to make that mistake again. "Run it again. Never mind, I'll run it through the Ranger database."

"Already did that. No nurse by that name at Brownsville. Look, I know that's right because all the medical people are in the authorized emergency response database and her name is not there. But I did find that there's an emergency room triage supervisor by that name. Since you don't believe in coincidences, they are most likely the same person."

Now I was confused. Why would Trich lie to Mark? While I was pondering the possibilities, Angella continued, "She appears to be the daughter of the Matamoras headman in the Southwest Group or whatever they're called. Part of the Gulf Cartel I believe. He is thought to control the drug traffic coming across the border through Brownsville."

"Now that's an interesting twist. Daughter of the drug lord gets close to the head of the Coast Guard station. How convenient! I think we'll rearrange the priorities of what the Chief suggested we do. Malcolm and her husband will just have to wait until we run Trich to ground." The puzzled look told me that Angella hadn't been briefed. "I'll bring you up to speed in the car. We're going over to Brownsville and pay Patricia May Rodriguez Santiago, AKA Trich, a visit. She has some explaining to do."

NINETEEN

We walked up the steps to Mark's room and, when we turned into the hallway from the stairwell, Trich was standing in the hall outside Mark's room talking to a man.

I froze and put my hand out for Angella to do the same. I instinctively reached down to my side and came up empty. Since neither of us had jackets we had left our firearms in the car. Not a good time to be naked. Actually, there are rules against leaving weapons in cars, but those rules are winked at for the most part.

I couldn't get a clear look at the man's face Trich was talking with, but his build was unmistakable, and he was hunched forward exactly as the tail had been when I caught him off balance trying to change directions. I was convinced this was the person who had been following us.

They spoke for a few more seconds, and then the man hurried away in the opposite direction. I toyed with the thought of chasing after him but didn't see a payoff in doing so. Trich was our immediate target. If she was working for the other team we'd soon get to the bottom of it.

"Who was that?" I asked when we approached Trich, hoping to catch her off guard.

A bright smile spread across her face. She glanced at Angella, nodded, and continued, "Got great news! Doctor said Mark's chemistry is good, and his responses are all normal. They stick a sharp needle in his arms and legs at various places to test nerve response. All good."

"That's good news, indeed. But tell me, who was that?"

"I don't really know. I think he's the one we saw at the airport, the one you asked me about, but I'm not sure now."

"What makes you unsure?" I asked, watching her eyes for any telltale signs of stress. "What's different?"

"Nothing, But he said he's a buddy of Mark's, wants to know how he's doing. Wanted to know if he's awake, can he talk? He left when I said Mark would be in a coma until noon tomorrow."

"Trich, please call me immediately if you see him again. He's not a friend of Mark's."

A deep frown, almost on the verge of panic, spread across her face. "I will," she said, "I hope I didn't do anything wrong in talking about Mark. You got me worried about him." Then her face brightened again. "Hey, I have some more good news for you. My friend works with ultrasound. That's what they use to see babies before they're born. She said she'll come by after work," Trich checked her watch, "You're in luck, that's about now. She said she can look inside to see if that thing is there."

I glanced over to Angella who stood passively, her face giving nothing away. "Trich, this is Angella. Trich's full name is Patricia May Rodriguez Santiago." Smiling at Trich, I asked, "Did I get that right?"

"You did."

I didn't bother to explain why Angella was with me. I was content to allow Trich's imagination to fill in the blanks.

The two women shook hands.

I could hear Nora talking to Mark, her voice carrying all the way into the hall. "Can we wait out here until my friend arrives? I don't want to disturb Nora," Trich asked.

Trich led the way to an alcove, where several small tables were positioned, each surrounded by wooden chairs. "Not very comfortable," she commented, "but at least we can sit. There's a vending machine if you want something and coffee at the nurse's station.

"Nothing now, thanks. What about you?" I asked, looking at Angella.

She shook her head.

It had already been a long day, and it felt good to be off my feet. A low-grade throb had started in my shoulder on the drive from South Padre. "Trich," I began, "what department do you work in? Did Mark say emergency room? I don't recall."

She immediately looked away, her right hand involuntarily coming up to cover the lower part of her face. Tears welled in her eyes. Without looking at me she said, "I have something to confess. I wanted to say this earlier but didn't. I work in the emergency department, but I'm not a nurse. I coordinate incoming patients before they see a nurse. It's called triage."

I focused on her face, my eyes communicating displeasure. After a long moment I asked, "So just exactly why does Mark believe you're a nurse? Did you tell him you were a nurse?"

More tears. She fumbled in her bag for a tissue and wiped her cheeks. Black smudges formed at the corners of her eyes and streaked when the tears continued.

Again we waited for her to settle on her story. The woman was at least a good actress, because the tears seemed genuine and the shortness of breath lent an air of true personal tragedy.

Angella remained quiet, as we both waited for her to compose herself. This was a scene that had played out in front of me more times than I cared to remember. But to Angella this was a new experience, but she remained calm, waiting.

Trich was taking time to compose what she wanted us to know and I only hoped it was going to be the truth.

She sucked in a deep breath, just as I had coached my son to do back when he was in little league before delivering a critical pitch. Trich had been well coached.

"I'm sorry. I'm so very sorry," she finally began, her Mexican accent now very pronounced. I had to strain to understand all her words. "I'm in love with Mark; you must know this. He assumed I was a nurse when I first met him. He was so upset when his friend came here, like he was a brother or even a son." She again wiped her eyes, and the black lines extended even further. "We got along right away, and I saw him in the lunch room and we had coffee together. Things went from there. I was afraid he would not like me if he thought I was an office employee so I never told him."

"And you planned to marry him? Not exactly a good beginning."

"I love him so much. He's the best man I ever knew."

"When were you going to tell him the truth? You know he'd find out sooner or later."

"I kept trying to do it. He was afraid to take me to his mother, because I'm a National as he called me. But he kept saying that when she knew I was a nurse, she would be okay with me. I didn't want to lose him, so I said nothing."

Her performance was superb. Would have fooled me, except for her father. Chance meeting with Mark or planned? The drug trade was big business with lots of smart people running their operations. They couldn't bring a thousand tons of cocaine a year into the United States if dummies ran the show. They very easily could have arranged for one of Mark's men to be injured, knowing full well Mark would visit the hospital. From there, it was the well-traveled story of boy meets girl.

For now, I was willing to play along with the masquerade. Was she searching for the file because I asked her to or because the tail told her to find it? I was now more convinced than ever that something big was going down involving the Coast Guard. Trich's job before Mark was injured could have been to neutralize the SPI Coast Guard operation. I didn't yet know how they planned to make that happen.

Now that a new commander was in place, someone had to be assigned to take him out. I made a mental note to find out who was now in charge.

Trich turned to see who was approaching. The woman wore a light pink gown and carried a small bag. "Oh, Trich, I'm so sorry!" she exclaimed, "I thought he was through the worse of it." She put the bag down and threw her arms around Trich, pulling her out of the seat. "I'm so sorry."

Trich, realizing that her friend was reacting to her streaked face, stepped back and said, "It's not Mark! Thank God, he's still alive. I must look a mess. I'll go wipe my face. This is Jimmy, Mark's friend. The one I told you about. Jimmy, this is Eileen. She's going to do the sonogram. This is Jimmy's friend," she said looking toward Angella."

Angella stood. "Hi, I'm Angella."

"I'll be right back," Trich said, rushing off to the women's room.

"This is most unusual," Eileen said. "Usually, it's a child swallowed a toy or something. Old folks do that too. But not someone his age."

"Accidents happen, I guess," I replied.

"So what exactly am I looking for?"

"A flash drive is all I know. Don't know the size, nothing more. Sorry."

"Shape?"

"Don't know, but I assume like a small pencil. But it could be flat, don't know."

"If it's there, I'll find it. Digestion slows when they're in a coma so it can be anywhere really. Come in when you're ready, I'll get started."

"Have you known Trich a long while?" I asked, while she was setting up.

"Ever since she started. In fact, we both went through orientation together. That's how I first met her. She and Mark make a great couple, don't you think?"

"When was that? I mean, how long ago did you two start?"

"Four years in September. Time flies when you're having fun. Seems like yesterday. Well, excuse me, I'll get started."

"Where's the equipment?"

"In the bag. This is a new hand-held sonograph model. Works great. Developed for battlefield use, great in the ER. Finds all kinds of things fast."

Trich returned with a repaired face and she had added color to her cheeks. She was a pretty woman, dark complexioned if she had been American, but as a National she was actually fair skinned.

Nora was sitting in a chair off to the side, and I went over to talk with her while Eileen wiped a jelly substance on Mark's belly. "I don't know why I bothered to warm it, he can't feel it anyhow," Eileen said, as she brought the small hand device against his skin. The device looked like an electric razor with a curved end against his body. It had a small screen on a flat surface and I could see some cloudy images floating on and off the screen.

She worked the device back and forth across his stomach, gradually moving it downward. "Not in the stomach," she announced after a while. "Before we go lower, let's look in his esophagus."

A few minutes later, she said, "Esophagus clear. Now for the intestines and colon." She pulled the cover down farther and opened his gown even more, being carful to keep him modestly covered. She spread more of the gel substance and continued moving the probe increasingly lower. The gray images came and went from the screen and seemed to dance around uncontrollably.

"Nothing down here," she finally said. She put the probe down and began wiping his body dry. When she was satisfied, she said, "Please help me turn him on his side."

I moved forward to help and Nora started crying when I let go of her hand. "He's going to be just fine," I assured Nora, not being so sure myself.

"What are you going to scan now," I asked, when we had Mark positioned on his right side. "All I see are clouds moving across the screen."

"If I were scanning for a tumor or an organ, or for that matter, a fetus, I'd go slower and use different resolution. This device will show small changes in tissue density. It sends sound waves into the tissue, and they bounce off the organs. Different densities yield different images. You can understand that the differences between the density of a healthy organ is not that much different than the density of a tumor, so you can imagine the sensitivity this little puppy has. That's why a metal object will leap off the screen. Its density is magnitudes different. Believe me, if it's there we won't miss it."

"So, where are you looking now?"

Upper rectum. The only place left if it's there at all." She glanced at the three other women in the room and said, "May I ask you all to leave for a few minutes. I can't do this and keep him modest."

Trich said, "Mrs. Cruses, let's go get something to eat. You must be starved." Trich took Nora by the hand and helped her up. The two women left the room together, and I heard Nora say, "I can't eat; my boy is in there. I can't leave."

"He'll be fine," Trich replied, "while we go down and get some soup. They have good soup here. You have to keep your strength up for him."

"All right, if you insist. But let's make this quick."

Angella followed them into the hall and posted herself outside the door, watching as Trich and Nora made their way to the elevator.

Eileen pulled Mark's gown completely open and repeated the gel routine. She then brought the probe to bear against his lower back and slowly moved it down to his tailbone. The gray clouds again billowed across the screen as the probe moved. Obviously the images meant something to Eileen, but to me, it seemed as though the machine was acting randomly. I again expressed that thought.

"Oh, the machine is working. Mark has a couple of kidney stones of no real consequence, and his liver is normal. His bladder is working properly also." She smiled a mischievous smile and said, "And I can say without any doubt that he's not with child."

"I should hope not," I replied, going along with her humor, which served its purpose by breaking the tension.

"Ah!" she exclaimed, "there it is!"

The small screen had come alive. Eileen had been right; the flash drive was solid bright white and appeared to be about an inch, inch and a quarter, long and about a quarter of an inch across.

She pointed to faint lines on the screen. "That's the rectum at the very bottom end. The object is about ten centimeters into the rectum."

"When will it pass?"

"Can't say. Maybe in an hour. Maybe in a day. It's only about two centimeters, one inch, away from passing, but he's in a coma. Normally, when the rectum fills, the brain sends a signal to empty it. But in his condition it's anyone's guess."

She had me continue to hold him on his side, while she removed the gel and gently dried him. Then she repositioned his gown, and we turned him onto his back.

"Is there any way to...to induce the drive?"

"I'm not qualified to answer that. And I certainly am not allowed to do anything to make it happen."

"But if you could do something to make it pass, what would that something be?"

"I could lose my license. I can't be part of that."

I flashed my ID and said, "This is important. It could save his life."

"Is that a police badge?"

"Texas Rangers."

"Oh, my. I won't get in trouble if I tell you will I?"

"It'll remain between us," I promised. But as things were progressing, I wondered how long it would be before word got out.

"Okay, I trust you," she replied. "If I wanted it out I'd fold his legs up toward his chest and press down. That'll put pressure on the rectum and may expel the drive. Do it a few times and if it doesn't work that's it." She turned and left without another word.

Angella came in the room. I told her we had found the drive. She asked, "So what are you going to do? Wait?"

I winked. "Nothing else we can do. How about getting me some coffee while I wait?"

She started to protest, then thought better of it and disappeared down the hall.

"Okay, Mark, my young friend, I hate to do this to you, but it's better than some thug coming in tonight and cutting you open." I bent his legs upward, placed my hands where Eileen said to place them and pushed.

Nothing.

Pushed again.

Still nothing.

Third time's a charm I told myself.

Still nothing.

"I'm not finished yet my friend. That sucker's coming out." I pulled on gloves from a box on the table and turned him on his side.

One more push before I manually tried to extract the drive.

Nothing happened.

I again pushed his legs as hard as I could and held them there with his knees pressing into his intestines.

Still nothing changed.

I held his legs with my weak left arm and reached my hand down getting ready to probe with my gloved finger. I hesitated when Angella walked back into the room. I didn't want her involved. If something went wrong this had to be all on me.

I released his legs and pulled up the covers. She put the coffee on the table, and I said, "Thanks, but I think you forgot the cream."

"You drank it black the other night."

"That was night time. This is evening time. Just please get the cream." She looked at my gloved hands and then at Mark, shook her head and rolled her eyes. Then off she went.

Okay, I told myself, *time to get this over with*. I squirted lubricant on my fingers just as my doctor had done during my last physical when he checked my prostrate. I pulled his legs up in preparation for retrieving the drive, pressed them toward his spine and reached down.

Mark's body tensed when I touched his rectum and my hand instantly moved away. I tried again and this time his sphincter tightened and a mass of hard-packed feces forced its way partially out and hung there suspended. Another contraction and the brown mass moved out further and, with a little help, fell into my gloved hand. I let out my breath when another nodule of shit broke free.

There it was!

The device I was looking for was barely visible, buried within the second mass. A few more knee pushes and it all fell free.

I extracted the device and wrapped the feces in my gloves, disposing of the whole mess in a box labeled 'hazardous materials'. Mark had encased the drive in a sealed plastic case and I used the room sink to clean it.

When Angella returned I was sipping my coffee.

"What about the cream?" she asked, shaking her head and looking over at Mark who was again lying on his back, the sheet pulled up to his shoulders.

Smiling, I answered, "I decided it's night. I don't need the cream after all."

TWENTY

We were on the way back to the island and I asked Angella if she wanted to catch a bite to eat.

"I'm always ready to eat," she replied. "What do you have in mind?"

"That place where Joy Malcolm hangs out. The place we met last night. Or was that two nights ago? I lost track."

"You mean *Louie's*. You really want to eat, or are you hoping to catch up with her?"

I wondered if I detected a bit of, shall I call it, jealousy. "What's wrong with killing two birds—so to speak?"

"Nothing. I just wanted to understand the agenda."

We drove in silence, both of us avoiding the topic of the drive I had retrieved.

"Crossing the bridge back onto the island, Angella suggested that we eat at the *Sea Ranch* and then go to *Louie's* afterward. "The *Sea Ranch* is one of my favs," she had explained, "don't get to go there often and frankly, it would be nice to go off duty for a while."

So we did just what Angella suggested. What can be bad about sitting at water's edge, across from a lovely woman, and having a wonderful meal?

We did just that and two hours later we headed over to *Louie's*. The timing was perfect. I could hear Joy long before I saw her. She was at the bar in the same spot as before. Only this time, her husband was nowhere to be seen. The other friends were the same. Apparently, they had been there a while. Joy was as high tonight as she had been the last time, but the volume of her voice was higher. There was an excitement in her, nervousness almost. She was telling a fishing mishap story that seemed to go on and on.

"Jimmy!" she exclaimed when she saw us come through the door. "Come join the party. You're a friend. Bring your lady cop friend with you; we'll clean up our act so we won't get arrested. Right everybody?" She laughed.

The others with her were less than thrilled, but no one expressed any disagreement. Angella passed me a look that clearly said, *I'll do this but it's not my idea of fun.* In our line of work most of what we did was not fun.

"Hey," Joy called to me, when I was still ten feet away. "I was right about Heart. He was murdered! It was no accident."

The fact that she knew this was troubling. To my knowledge, the public had not been informed. "I haven't heard that bit of information," I replied. "How do you know?"

"Got my sources. People tell me things."

"Could just be rumor, you know."

"Not this time. He was killed for certain."

"So you keep saying."

"I know!" she snapped. "It's official."

"Do you know who did it? Why?"

"That's not my department. That's hers." She pointed at Angella. "You should be out there hunting for clues, not hanging around in here with us drunks." She paused to laugh. Then raised her mug, and asked, "Hey, want a beer?"

"No thanks. We're set for now," I replied, a bit too quickly.

She winked in my direction. "Show the lady a good time, Jimmy. You might get lucky after all."

Angella's eyes tightened, but she held her ground and maintained her smile. "Speaking of getting lucky, where's your husband? He's the guy needs the luck."

"He used his luck up long ago—in every aspect." She laughed at her joke. "He won't be getting very lucky for a long while. See you in the gym." She turned back to her friends. We had been dismissed.

Angella whispered, "You ask me, she's jealous. She wants you."

"Woman's got a problem. She wants anything with pants. Don't know what her sleeping arrangements are, but she's always on the make."

"It's okay by me, if you want to score, go score. As you said, kill a couple of birds."

"Let's go order a drink. We can deal with Joy in the morning. Besides, it's her husband we need to scope, not her."

As was Angella's habit, she ordered a Coke and I had a Miller. We sat nursing our drinks, listening to Joy and her friends getting higher and noisier by the minute. I was wondering when the bartender would cut them off when Joy's husband, John, appeared in the doorway. To say he was agitated is an understatement. He was taller than I had remembered and walked with a purpose. This was definitely the same man she had been with last night, but his demeanor was certainly different. I attributed it to his now being sober.

As soon as Joy realized her husband was approaching, she quieted down. The ambient noise level fell. Even her friends stopped talking.

He walked straight to where she had been holding forth, leaned close, and said something in her ear. Then he turned and made his way back toward the door.

I expected some smart-ass comment from Joy, but instead, she turned to her friends, and said, "Gotta go now. See ya," and proceeded across the floor and out the door following in her husband's footsteps.

"What do you make of that?" I asked Angella. "I expected her to bite his head off."

"No idea. The other night, he had to drag her out. Now she follows like a docile puppy."

"It doesn't add. Didn't she just get finished saying he wouldn't be getting lucky any time soon? And then she runs after him like a school girl in heat."

"I wouldn't know about the school girl in heat analogy," Angella replied, "but you're right, it doesn't add right."

"Let's go see what we can find out." I put money on the table and we slipped out, being careful to remain far enough behind them to avoid being spotted.

No car was leaving the parking area.

No cars were even moving on the street out front.

I pulled Angella back against the building, assuming they were somewhere close by having a conversation.

Angella tapped my arm. "There they are," she whispered, pointing to two figures walking quickly down a side street, heading toward the beach. Joy was moving faster than someone who had had as much to drink as she apparently had.

The possibility crossed my mind that Joy could have been acting. I said as much to Angella.

"Something about that woman is off," she replied. "She never
touched the beer the whole time we were there. Waved it around a
lot, but it never wet her lips."

We followed along, and when they turned north on Gulf Boulevard, the last street parallel to the beach, we waited until a car
came between us, and then we used the car as cover to cross over
Gulf. We maintained cover beside the parked cars, keeping about a
hundred yards south of where they were.

They walked past a series of what I would call rental houses,
built on stilts high enough to allow storm surges to wash under
them without causing damage. What would have been garages on
normal houses were, in fact, porticos open at front and back and
used primarily to store beach toys and boat trailers.

They stopped in front of a house that, judging from the pillars
underneath, must have once been painted green but had faded to
gray. They both looked around, as if trying to be sure no one was
watching. Then Joy followed her husband through the portico to the
back yard.

They were now both out of sight.

A few moments later, a light flashed on and off in a back room. I
guessed that to be the kitchen. We waited fifteen minutes, and nothing more happened. "Call it in, would you," I said to Angella. "We
shouldn't be out here without letting the desk know what's going on."

Angella glanced over at me, a look of concern spreading across
her face. It was the same look my son always had when he knew I
was about to be angry with him for doing something he should not
have done. Before I could ask her what her issue was, she sheepishly
said, "I called it in when we got here."

That's why she had been assigned to me. Chief Duran was taking no chances. My choice was to be angry with her and say something. Or be angry with her and keep my thoughts to myself. I chose to be quiet. Hey, there's still hope for me, right?

I crept up the street to see if I could get a better angle on the house. The view from there wasn't much better, so I returned to where Angella was posted. She knew what I had been thinking and said, "Truth is, I did it out of training, not thinking it through. I told them not to send a car unless they didn't hear from us in an hour. It seemed silly after I did it, so I didn't say anything."

"No secrets," I admonished. "If we're to work together, then we coordinate with each other. Is that clear?" That was the wrong thing to say. She studied me a long while, obviously making up her mind how she wanted to handle the disk I had taken from Mark without telling her.

She finally replied, "That cuts both ways you know."

It was my turn to apologize. "Ok, you made your point, but no more—either way. Now, tell the desk to watch the house all night. We need to know when they leave and where they go. Tell them to send someone who can do this without observation. We'll wait here until they're on station. Also tell them not to approach but to capture on video."

"Can't believe this," she said, when she snapped her phone closed. "Chief authorized the watch with no cross-examination, no nothing. Thought we'd have a hard time, but no. Guess you got some stroke."

"When was the last time you had two open murder investigations down here?"

"Can't recall any stories of even one."

"That give you your answer? Chief's not going home 'till this is resolved. He's sleeping up there. This is twenty-four-seven for him. At least now he has something to watch. Some action going."

"Looks like it could be that way for us also."

"It very well could be."

Ten minutes later, Angella's cell buzzed. She read the text message: **On station. 100 ft north of you. Good view.**

We were walking back to where we had left the car, when Angella's cell announced: **Man and woman leaving house. Going south towards you. We'll follow.**

We ducked behind a parked car and watched. It was Joy and her husband and they passed on the other side of the street. A few minutes later, an unmarked car made its way down the street. When the couple turned west back toward Louie's, the car continued and turned down a parallel street.

We stayed low for several more minutes, giving them plenty of time to clear the area. At this point, they were being followed by the stakeout team and weren't our responsibility.

I wondered what they had been doing in that house at such a late hour with no lights on. Obviously, they were up to something, but nothing made any sense from what we knew.

Again Angella's sharp eyes came in handy. She pointed back toward the house where Joy had been, and I could just make out the silhouette of a man leaning against a pole under the portico.

Suddenly, a car turned the corner across from us, traveled north toward where the man was standing and stopped directly across the street. The man under the house ran across the street passing in front of the waiting car. The instant he was in the headlamps of the waiting car, we both knew immediately who it was.

I reached for the non-existent Beretta and Angella pulled out her cell phone and immediately sent the text: **All units follow car now going north on Gulf in front of target home. Paco is in car. Have a car pick us up.**

One thing I can say for the Chief is that he runs a tight operation. A marked car came by in less than a minute and the car that had been following Joy caught up to Paco's car about ten blocks north on Gulf.

Almost immediately the Chief's voice broke over the police radio. "Fifty-Two," that was the unmarked car, "follow at safe distance. Do not intercede. Seven," that was our car, "proceed to headquarters. Silent. Don't give targets reason to know we're onto them."

A few minutes later, we were sitting on the second floor of City Hall listening to the unmarked's progress up the Island. It became clear that Paco was being driven back to his base on the sand.

The Chief leaned over, keyed his microphone, and said, "Fifty-two, drop back now. Any further and they'll spot you. I suppose they're going to change vehicles in about a mile. We'll let County take it from here."

He turned to a Sergeant who had been sitting off to the side. "Coordinate with County. Let them know Paco's back. They'll know what to do."

Chief Duran turned to me. It was two-thirty in the morning, and I had expected his face to show the grind. Instead, he looked as though he had just woken from a good night's rest. On the flip side, I had studiously avoided the mirrors in the rest room a few minutes earlier. "Nice work tracking down Paco. Now tell me what the hell you were doing at the hospital?"

"Visiting Mark."

"That all?"

I wondered how much Angella had texted and decided that she would not have told him about the flash drive. "And to check out his girl friend, Trich. Patricia May Rodriguez Santiago to be more accurate. Angella ran a name check and she turns out to be the daughter of a drug hotshot in Matamoras."

"So?"

"Do you mean what do I think? I don't know what to make of her. She seems honest, but she could be lying through her teeth. I can't get a good handle. Maybe 'cause I'm too close through Mark."

He turned to Angella. "You're take?"

She thought for a moment, before responding, choosing her words carefully. She knew her future depended on her performance during this assignment. "My reaction is she's telling the truth. I believe she's in love with him, and I agree that could color my impression. But she's a nice kid, and I think genuine."

Duran dug through a box of files on the table in front of him, and finding the one he wanted, threw it on the table. It was thicker than most of the others on the table and had several red tags extending out of the side. Seems Ms. Santiago had not escaped the attention of several organizations. The DEA has been watching her, as has Homeland Security, and even the FBI has been in on it. "This had been a routine investigation before she met Mark, being the daughter of someone on the watch list and coming into the country every day. When she started dating Mark, Homeland Security, actually the Coast Guard, got concerned and upped the stakes."

"So what's the bottom line?" I asked, trying not to get ahead of Duran.

"Bottom line is inconclusive." He looked from me to Angella and back to me. "Investigators deal in observations. Feelings count, and you've told me more than all the investigation over five years has. I tend to agree with you. They've found nothing of any importance, other than she lied to Mark about being a nurse. Not the first time a woman did that and certainly not the last."

Angella flashed him a look, but she apparently thought better of saying anything and turned toward me rolling her eyes.

I told Duran about the man who followed us and noted that he was the same person I saw talking to Trich in the hospital.

"Describe him," the Chief barked.

When I did, he flipped though the file and found a picture. "Is that the man?" he asked.

"That's him." I pushed the picture to Angella. "You agree?"

"That's him," she confirmed. "That's the man I saw talking to Trich at the hospital."

"Good news, anyway," he sighed. "He's with Homeland Security. At least that seems to be good news. It also seems to confirm your conclusion that Trich is not working for her father."

"Now we know we have two teams looking for the video. Homeland security and that guy who jumped me this morning. I'm putting him as a drug dealer."

"Get some rest, the both of you," Duran said. "There's little chance of a drug drop tonight. Too late for one thing and too much moon for the other. These things happen when it's dark. I estimate a few more days 'till they're ready to go again."

"Why not wait unto there's no moon?"

"Nature has a hand here. Around the full moon, the sharks like to feed close to shore. So, for about a week after that, the heat detectors, or motion detectors, or whatever technology the spooks are using to detect boat traffic, are thrown off by the sharks churning the water."

"Doesn't that hinder Paco and his gang being in the water?"

"Not unless you're a fish. These waters carry plenty of natural food for the sharks. What the hell they want with some tough skinned human? And what the hell chance does a shark have against a predator like Paco? Mutual respect. In any event, the sharks don't seem to slow him down."

"You're convinced then this is all about drugs."

"It's a good place to begin. Trace the money, you got the perp. Works every time."

"Think we should brief the Coast Guard just to be on the safe side," I suggested.

"Got that base covered already. Did that as a matter of course," Duran replied, matter of factly. I got the distinct impression he didn't appreciate my meddling.

"What did they say?"

"I didn't talk to them directly. What does that matter?"

"Since my encounter with Captain, what's his name? Getting late. Oh, Boyle. Captain Boyle, I've had the feeling the Coast Guard's got their nose in this thing for reasons we don't understand."

"Give me a minute." He fiddled, and after a few false starts, brought up a new screen on his computer. He spent several seconds typing commands or passwords and a time-log appeared on the screen. It seemed to be a display of every conversation his dispatcher had, showing both sides of the conversation. He scrolled down and found what he was looking for.

A puzzled look crossed his face. "This is indeed odd. The person who took our report was none other than your friend Boyle. Now what the hell's a Coast Guard Captain doing running the radio? I'm even surprised Boyle knows where the radio room is located. I don't know if they have buck-privates anymore, but I would think officers don't typically log in calls to the Coast Guard. They got to have radiomen for that purpose."

"The man's up to something, that's for sure. What did he actually say?"

The Chief read a bit further and then replied, "His exact words were, 'Got that Sergeant. It's in the logbook. But don't be expecting help on this. You'll have to go it alone, I'm afraid.' Nice guy, your friend."

"Sounds as though he has more important things on his mind," I commented. "Wonder what's going down."

"This is most unusual. What they normally do is dispatch a couple of patrol boats and try to disrupt the drop. We find if we can mess with their timing, we have a chance to intercept them, sometimes on the water, but usually on the beach. But these folks are sophisticated. They have underwater sensors, stuff like we have, so they know if we're lurking in the shallows with motorboats. And Paco, he's the best. Man can sense the law miles away. Don't know how he does it, but he's uncanny. If anything can get ashore he'll deliver it."

"So what's your take?" I asked the chief.

"I'd rather not say at this point. But I don't like it one bit. Go get some sleep. If anything breaks, I'll call you. You want it by text or voice?

"Text will work."

TWENTY-ONE

The cell phone text alert went off at five-thirty. By my calculations, I had slept two hours, maybe a little longer. It was from the Chief: **Warrant was issued to search house on Gulf. Scheduled for six. Your option to be there.**

How they had managed to obtain a warrant on the evidence that I knew about I couldn't imagine, but then again, I didn't have all the facts. I certainly didn't have the access to Judges that the Chief had. I quickly dressed and headed out. It was a six-minute drive from the TIKI to the house, so I had plenty of time.

When I arrived, Angella pulled up at almost the same time. There were two marked SPI police cars, one marked truck, and several generic vans. The Chief was sitting in an unmarked Buick.

He signaled for me to come over. "We got ourselves a full house. DEA, FBI, County. I keep looking up, half expecting Navy Seals. Maybe they plan to drop out of the sky or something. Just lay low and watch. I don't need for you to go in."

"What are you looking for?"

"That's just the thing. Don't know. Paco is on the beach. Maybe he left something behind."

I didn't want to inquire into the warrant and what they had told the judge. That was the Chief's business. "Guys like Paco seldom leave a trail. We'll be lucky to get so much as a finger print."

"Never know. That's what makes this job so interesting."

Angella came over, and I quickly briefed her. She was wearing a jacket and I guessed she now had her gun with her as I had. No more Mr. Soft Touch.

The Chief motioned to his back seat and I retrieved two protective vests and handed one to Angella. She had never worn one, so I helped her into it, being careful to keep my fingers where they belonged.

At five fifty-five the team, some of whom appeared to be women, assembled beside a blue van. They were all dressed in dark coveralls and carrying various lethal weapons, all pointed straight up. They listened intently to their final orders and, on command, ran to their stations, positioning themselves at each door and under each window. They were all wearing hearing devices. Almost in unison, they snapped off their safeties. I knew from times past that this was the dangerous period. With adrenalin pumping, anything could happen. Here is where training and discipline came together.

I motioned Angella to come with me, and we positioned ourselves behind the team. I planned to follow them through the front door. I couldn't hear their instructions, but I could see their eyes and was ready to move when they did.

From Angella's wide-eyed look, I was certain this was her first home invasion. She was rightly tense. These missions were inherently dangerous, especially if we caught an armed scoundrel by surprise. Friendly fire—only a PR genius could have coined such a term—was always a concern. This was especially true when different law enforcement organizations came together infrequently. We had the perfect storm going for us this morning and I was concerned, especially for Angella.

At exactly six, the lock was blown from the front door of the small house and I assume the same thing happened in the rear. Nobody said a word, but the four-person team in front of us ran forward into the house and immediately spread out, clearing lines of fire.

Angella and I stepped in behind them and positioned ourselves on either side of the front door. We could see the team from the back race through the kitchen, checking the panty and opening each closet. One person positioned herself outside a small bathroom and nodded her head. Another man pushed the door open.

Meticulously, they cleared the first floor. Even the refrigerator had been checked and cleared. This team was well trained and thorough.

Now for the hard and dangerous part, the second floor. There was only one way up and anyone going up the steps was an easy target from above.

Two men with helmets and face gear rushed to the base of the stairs and paused. When nothing happened, they raced up the steps two at a time. The house was silent.

Three men and a woman followed in their footsteps. Suddenly, the silence was broken. "Front room, two men," said the man next to me for our benefit. "Also, right side back room, one man."

Several more assault team members raced up the steps. I put my arm out indicating for Angella to remain where she was. Now that we knew the house had occupants, anything could happen. They didn't require us upstairs, we'd just mess up the shooting angles.

A window was smashed, and two gunshots rang out from the second floor, followed by shouts from outside. Then the sound of feet running across the floor echoed on the first floor, followed by several loud thuds, as though furniture was being thrown to the floor.

"They need help outside," the man next to me said. I ran out in time to see two men leap from the second floor window and land on top of a uniformed man on the ground. A third man leaped on top of the pile, bounced to his feet, and ran toward the beach, less than a block away.

Angella and I ran after him. He was small, wiry—and fast. The distance between us was increasing. Angella was slightly ahead of me, but I was holding my own. I made a mental note to thank Teran for the leg training.

The perp hit the sand at full speed and two steps in, his right foot slid sideways and he fell to his knees. That allowed us to gain on him. Even though we did not have our guns drawn, the terror on his face was evident.

He was barefoot and dressed only in his underwear. He pushed himself upright and his feet regained traction and off he went. Angella had to stop to remove her shoes and, in that instant it became clear that neither of us were going to catch him.

I yelled, "Stop, Police! Stop or I will shoot."

Angella pulled her gun and leveled it at the back of his head. I reached out and pushed her arm down.

"What did you do that for?" she squealed. "I had him in my sight!"

"I'm on leave because I killed a man doing just what you were about to do."

"That's insane."

"Trouble is, with this scumbag we don't even know why he's running. For all we know, they broke into the wrong house. We were looking for Paco. That's not him. Imagine if you kill an innocent person."

"He's running from us. You told him to stop. That's enough."

"Maybe for the law. But not for the press. They'll hang you out to dry."

"That's insane." This was the first time I saw any semblance of passion in her, and even then it was fairly mild.

"My guess is, judging from the look on his face, he's terrified. I bet he's here illegally."

"Looked oriental."

"Korean if you ask me. Possibly Japan, something like that. Press'd have a field day if you shot him. Profiling and all."

"The world's upside down, all I can say." She pulled out her radio and called in his description. I heard her say. "Perp's heading north from Beach Access nine wearing only grey underwear. Five-three, about one hundred ten maybe twenty pounds, light skinned, dark hair. Oriental, possibly Korean or Vietnamese. We are not, re-peat not, in pursuit."

She clicked off and commented, "They've dispatched three pa-trols onto the beach. Can't get far in his undies. Hard to blend in."

"Nothing's for certain with these types. Take it from experi-ence. Let's get back to the house and see what they have."

The number of law enforcement vehicles seemed to have quadrupled. Red and blue flashing lights were spread out for two hundred yards on either side of the house and down both feeder streets. Cars exclaiming Sheriff, Constable. Cameron County, State Trooper, Border Patrol, ATF, and DEA were interspersed at every conceivable angle. None of them would be able to leave until they all decided to go. I also knew from the earlier briefing that FBI agents were in the mix, but I didn't immediately see any evidence of their presence.

Three men were lying face down on the sand in front of the building, their hands cuffed behind them. I glanced over to the

Chief's car and noted he was in a heated discussion with a man that looked to be twice his size.

Chief Duran was standing outside his car and the other man was towering over him, while several SPI uniformed officers stood a few feet away. One of them had his right hand on his holster and I had the impression that all the Chief had to do was nod and the big fellow would find himself stopping a bullet. I only hoped the officer would wait for the nod.

The Chief succeeded in calming the big man long enough for the two of them to climb into his car and close the door. After about five minutes, the car doors opened and both men got out. The intensity in the Chief's eyes had eased. The officer with the itchy trigger finger relaxed but kept his eyes focused on the big man. The Chief walked over to his officer, said something I could not hear, and the man, with a last nasty glance over his shoulder, moved off to issue orders to several other SPI uniforms. The three men in handcuffs were put in separate cars.

The big man waved a hand to someone and, immediately, several cars backed away, and the tangle of vehicles slowly began to disperse. It was another five minutes or so before the three cars in which the prisoners were seated were able to drive away from the house.

Angella had been off to the side, listening to police communications. Apparently, they had our beach target cornered, as he tried to make his way down a side street a half-block from the beach. She motioned for me to come over. I heard the radio say, "We're moving in. Guy's got his hands over his head. Wearing only brown underwear. Hispanic male, five eight or nine, two twenty."

Angella grabbed the radio from the officer next to her, keyed the mike and shouted, "Negative that! Perp's five three, five four at most, no more than one thirty. Wearing *grey* underwear. Asian Definitely not Hispanic!"

The reply came back immediately. "This one's in his undies, over two hundred. Hispanic."

"Wrong guy!" Angella replied. "Asian. Small man. No more than five three or four!" The officer next to her snickered.

The radio came alive, the professional voice now sarcastic and irritated. "How the hell many guys are there on the beach running around in their skivvies?" Everyone within earshot of the radio burst out laughing. Not that it was so funny, but it broke the tension.

Angella didn't respond. There was nothing more she could report.

Then the speaker said, "Target's cuffed. Claims he works for City Utilities picking up trash. Says a skinny guy jumped him, held a gun to the back of his head and made him take off his clothes. Stole the truck and his clothes."

"Gun?" Angella responded. "Check if he's sure it was a gun?"

A moment later the answer came back. "Man says it could have been a stick or a rock, he never saw it. The perp was wild, talking in a language he didn't understand."

"Which way did the truck go?"

"South," came the reply a few seconds later.

Just then the police dispatcher broke in. "All available units, City Utility truck reported driving south on the beach at a high rate of speed. Driver is a small, oriental male. He accosted a seventy-year-old male, took his shirt and shorts. Shirt is light blue, shorts are gray. Vehicle going south."

Sirens immediately filled the air as almost every car that had been at the house joined the chase. How hard could it be to catch a garbage truck?

I walked over to Chief Duran, who started to say something, and then broke it off when a report came in on his radio.

"Shit," he exclaimed, "they found the truck down by Schlitter-bahn. Abandoned. No sight of the target. They're looking for a man wearing a blue shirt and gray shorts, but I hold little hope we'll get him. He's obviously highly trained and knows his way around."

"What was that about before?" I asked Duran, curious about the earlier heated exchange. "I mean that big guy and you were going at it pretty good."

Duran moved closer. "Asshole's lucky I didn't shoot his dick off," he said, his voice barely above a whisper. "Accident of course. He's with INS. One of those low life's we busted in that house was a plant, one of his men. That house was being used to smuggle il-legals into the country. He had it infiltrated. Only thing is, he's got to register with us when he works our territory. Claims there's a friggin' leak in my department, and he was tired of losing these guys, so he was playing this close to the chest. That's when I should have let him have it!"

I had no intention of getting myself mixed up in local politics. I couldn't begin to count the times we did work in jurisdictions with-out informing the locals, especially when it seemed that the bad guys were getting the jump on us. So I asked, "Illegals from what country? Do we know where they're coming from?"

"Mexico, primarily."

"The guy on the beach isn't Mexican. He stole the truck and the driver couldn't understand him."

"What do you make of that?" Duran asked, clearly frustrated by the turn of events. And judging from our few encounters, he was pissed that his people had caught the wrong naked guy.

"Haven't put it together yet, but now we have a tie among Paco, the Malcolms, and now some Asian type. I think we should focus on the Malcolms."

"Go for it. I got to get back to deal with the mess this has stirred up. FBI will weigh in any minute. I'm surprised they haven't already."

"Probably asked to stand down, like the Governor was."

"Yes, but *why's* my question. FBI never steps down. They're worse than your bunch! If there's something going down, those A holes will be in the mix!"

"You sure they're not here?"

"For all I know, the Navy seals showed up! This frigging thing's out of control, and I don't like that one bit!"

Angella chose that moment to walk over.

"Why the hell didn't you plug him when you had a chance?" Duran snapped at her. "Woulda saved me a lot of grief!"

Angella shrugged and glanced at me, her eyes saying it all.

Before I could come to her rescue, Duran added, "Just letting off steam. The last thing in the world I need now was another person shot. But you'd think we could catch a naked guy running on the beach!"

"You'd think," I responded.

Duran shot me a look that said I had exceeded my welcome.

Angella grabbed my elbow and steered me toward my car. The look on her face clearly telling me it was time to get out of Dodge.

TWENTY-TWO

"**O**kay, now what?" Angella asked, as the last of the law enforcement cars pulled away, leaving behind the inevitable
curious neighbors. "It seems all we do is follow people around, and
when something happens, they slip through our fingers."

"Welcome to the world of investigation. As they say, we spend
long hours of boredom interspersed with high bursts of adrenalin."

"I don't picture you bored. Not after all the years you've been
doing this. You got a chance to get out, move on to something else,
yet you want back."

"I'm not bored. Just a saying. I'm not good at anything other
than what I do. Some guys like a desk, like the indoors. Drives me
nuts. I've got to be free to come and go as I wish. Figuring things
out from tiny bits of information gets me going. Speaking of information, let's check out the owner of the apartment where the OD
guy was found."

"I'm sure that was done already. Should I pull the report?"

"We'll do it ourselves. That's another of my traits. Unless I do it in person, I'm suspicious of what's on the paper. Some folks never see beyond what they are told. I read the scene as well as the inform- ant, draw my own conclusions. But, yes, get the report. Also, see what the report says about where he works." I checked my watch. "Hey. It's still early, only eight; let's catch him before he leaves for work. Unless, of course, you want to get something to eat first."

"Got to let the adrenalin settle. I never came that close to pull- ing the trigger before. If I try to eat now, I might just lose it." An- gella fell silent for a while and then said, "You know, when I'm on the firing range, I often ask myself if I would really be able to pull the trigger."

"Well, what's the verdict?"

"I think I would have, but do you ever really know before you actually do it? I know I delayed a bit, told myself I wanted to get a clean shot. I'll never know now if I would have or not."

"In life or death, I mean your own life or death, you know what you'll do. When it's either you or the perp, you'll pull it every time. When they're running away, when their back's to you, that's an- other story indeed."

"Have you ever been in that situation? I mean when you shot a man when he was just trying to get away and your own life was not in danger?"

Here it was. The question that was at the heart of my leave. The question the investigation board had tried to come to grips with. If it had not been for the fact that my own shoulder had stopped a bullet I would have been indicted for manslaughter. The evidence showed that Badman Tex had his back turned when the bullet struck him. He had been running away. The question was never answered as to whether my own partner had saved my ass by firing his spare gun into my shoulder and then planting it on Badman. I was not about to resolve the issue now. "Not that I recall," I replied, fading the question.

"Not that you recall!" What kind of bull-crap answer is that? Either you did or you didn't."

"Nothing in life is a simple yes or no. You should know that."

"What are you alluding to?"

"Your marriage. What did you do that would make your husband file for divorce? But he did. Not all things have straightforward answers."

"Jimmy, one thing I'll say about you, you divert well. And you know how to hurt even better. You're dodging the question, why I don't know. But I thought we had a trust thing going here. Let's just drop the subject before you and I aren't speaking."

My cell beeped. It was Trich: **Come ASAP. Mark's awake and needs you immediately.**

I responded: **On my way.**

I turned my car back toward City Hall. "Here's the choice. I'm going to the hospital to see Mark; he's awake and needs to see me. You can come or you can visit the neighbor yourself."

"My assumption is you want to be alone with Mark. I don't see how interviewing a teacher is any problem. And besides, a little private time will do us both a bit of good."

I parked next to her car. She opened the door and stepped out, still quietly seething. The question she had asked was painful and potentially incriminating. For all I knew, the question had been presented to her by Chief Duran to help out the State. I wouldn't put it past my boss to set it up this way. "Before you go, I need to put your cell into my phone. I suggest you do the same."

We exchanged numbers, and I said, "A few keys. Cap H means I'm in trouble and need help immediately. Cap HS means I'm in trouble but don't approach. S for stay away."

"That's it?"

"Lonnie and I, that's my partner, Lonnie Turner, have a whole list of codes. These two will do for now."

"I should be back on the Island by eleven, noon at the latest. See you then." I turned off the engine and when she gave a puzzled look, I said, "Gotta use the men's room. See you later."

- - - - -

I made good time to Brownsville and arrived just at nine o'clock. My cell phone rang, and it was the TIKI reporting a break-in in my room. The security guard saw two guys forcing the door, and when he checked he found them going though my stuff. He called it in to the SPI police and watched from a safe distance. They took nothing that he could see.

A moment later the call came from Chief Duran. "Seems you're a popular guy around these parts. A couple of men tossed your room. Anything of value you have there is probably gone."

"Nothing. Have my watch and wallet. Maybe it's the guy from the beach looking for something to wear. Hope he didn't take my best jeans."

"You poking fun at us?" he replied, not at all amused by my sense of humor. "You're the guy who lost him on the beach, I wouldn't be talking if I was you."

"I should have let Angella put a forty-five through his head. Then you wouldn't have lost a truck."

"They'd have my job over that, and yours as well. The guy's from North Korea, that much we now know. Where the hell are you?"

I told him what I was doing, and he replied, "Get that done with and get back over here. I'm not comfortable having Angella without back up. She's too green for this alone. This thing is messy enough. Don't need one of my men, ah, or women, down."

The implication was that it was okay for me to go down. I was the State's problem, and they could handle the heat anyway they wanted. But one of his was too close to home. "I'll make it as fast as I can," I said into a dead line.

I took the steps two at a time and raced down the hall. I was hoping to spot Trich, and when I didn't see her, I assumed she was in the room with Mark.

The door was closed. I pulled it open and stepped inside. In the instant before an arm locked tight against my windpipe I noted that both beds were empty.

Two men had been waiting behind the door. One of them now had a forearm pressing hard against my windpipe. I was fighting for air and not succeeding very well. The other man had slipped a belt around my body pinning my arms to my side.

Professionals of some sort without a doubt. Efficient professionals.

"You can make this easy or difficult," One of them said. "Your choice. Where is it?"

"What?" I managed to cough out, the words using up what little air I had left.

"You know exactly what! The flash drive, that's what! We know you have it. Don't make this tough on yourself."

"Screw you," I tried to say, but it came out something like, "Smoo ouh."

"I hope that's not what I think you said," the guy clamping my neck said, pressing even harder against my throat.

My head went light and my knees became wobbly. I tried to move my hand toward my gun but it was impossible to move.

The other man was going through my pockets, working his way down from my jacket to my slacks. He was throwing things on the floor as he went. First my keys, then some change, followed by sunglasses, money clip, wallet, cell phone, some receipts, more change, a pen.

"A gun!" he exclaimed. "What the hell!" He unclipped the leather strap holding it in the holster and slipped it out. "A Berretta no less." He expertly emptied the chamber and placed the gun on the bed. He then reached around and removed the extra cartridge case from the gun belt. He dumped the bullets into his pocket along with the ones he had emptied from the Berretta. He threw the empty case on top of the gun.

"Nothing else here," he announced. "Where the hell is it?"

I couldn't have answered even if I was willing.

Sensing this, the pressure on my throat eased and I gasped for air. My lungs hurt as they partially filled. My throat was already swelling from the bruising.

"Where's the file?" The question came again.

"Don't have it." The arm around my throat tightened even more than before and I thought I felt something pop. The belt was pulled tighter and my fingertips went numb.

"Listen asshole. You got the file and we'll get it, it's just a matter of time. You want to stay healthy, you cooperate. We're serious. Give over the file and we're out of here."

The pressure on my throat again eased and I was able to take several deep breaths. I managed to again tell them I didn't have it.

"You got it all right and we intend to find it." He lit a match, pulled a cigarette from his jacket pocket, and sucked on it to create a red glowing ash.

I knew what was coming next and was in no position to prevent it.

"Okay, asshole, give it up now and save yourself permanent damage."

"You win," I pleaded, "I'll tell you. Give me air so I can talk." I was stalling for time, as I worked on the *horse might talk* theory of postponing the inevitable.

I took several breaths, my eyes firmly focused on the glowing cigarette end. "I left it in the car," I said.

The air was instantly cut off to my lungs.

The other man took a long inhale on the cigarette, making the ash glow bright orange. "It's not in that junk heap you call a car. We already tossed it! Last chance."

"I left it at——"

The fire alarm chose that instant to go off. The shrill was almost deafening, but was the best sound I had heard in years, ranking right up there with "My place or yours?"

Lights began to flash above the door and I knew they were flashing outside the room as well. From my knowledge of hospital security systems, the alarm was being repeated in every guard station in the hospital, every nurses station on the floor, as well as at the control center and directly at the fire and police stations. Funny how your mind works at times of stress, but I could visualize the fire trucks already being dispatched.

There is no time to delay with hospital fires. The patients can't just get up and walk out, so an army of first responders were rushing here. Automatic valves, I knew, had already closed off the oxygen and other combustible material lines and automatic containment doors had swung closed to partition off and isolate the fire.

In a moment or two, teams of first responders would be pouring through the door. These guys had forgotten that the smoke sensitivity in hospitals was set far lower than other places because of the inherent risk of explosion from the various gasses used. Nitrogen, pure oxygen, are not substances to fool with.

My captors realized this a bit too late. I was pushed to the floor as they both started for the door. The guy who had been clamping my neck now pulled back his right leg and I braced for the inevitable kick in the ribs.

His right foot started toward me. The motion was smooth, as if he had been a soccer player in another life. Suddenly, it became clear that he wasn't aiming for my ribs. His foot was moving with considerable force on a trajectory toward my unprotected groin. I had no time to roll out of the way. I moved my hands together as best I could to cushion the blow, but the strap limited my movement. I twisted slightly sideways but the target was still exposed.

I closed my eyes in anticipation of the pain. But it never materialized. His foot came to rest on top of my leg.

"Asshole! You owe me one!" He stepped over my cowering body and disappeared down the hall.

Within seconds, the room filled with responders. Several people held fire extinguishers and others had radios.

"What's going on in here?" a burly supervisor type fired a series of questions. What the hell are you doing on the floor? Where's the fire? Somebody been smoking?"

My neck ached and I was still gasping for breath. It felt as if my throat was permanently closed. I tried to talk, but my voice was high pitched and weak. Eventually, I said, "Two men. Don't let them get away."

"There's no one here but you. What's going on? You been smoking in here?"

I managed to pull myself into a sitting position and propped my back against the wall. Someone then realized by arms were bound and released the strap.

A nurse bent down to hear what I was saying and noticed the swelling. She exclaimed, "His neck's been injured. Get him flat; protect the neck. Code blue team. Stat. No more questions!"

I tried to push her away, but she said, "Do that again and I'll have you restrained. We need to immobilize your neck and get X-rays. It could be broken—or worse. Now lay still and we'll get you fixed up."

I tried to twist my head to show her it wasn't broken.

"If you ever want to walk upright again," she said, sharply, "you stay still for now! You sever the cord, we can't help you! Now do as I say and behave yourself."

The door flew open and several people came into the room, followed almost immediately by a gurney and two men wheeling heavy looking equipment bags.

A few seconds later, a bag inflated around my upper body and I couldn't move my head in any direction even if I had wanted to. I felt a prick on my right arm and realized an IV had been inserted. "Is that your gun on the bed," a male voice asked. "It's illegal to carry firearms in the hospital. Call security."

"I'm a Ranger," I tried to say, but it came out sounding like I was calling him a stranger.

A uniformed police officer arrived as they were lifting me onto the gurney. The last time this had happened, I had been lying in my own blood for twenty-minutes while my partner, Lonnie Turner, kept his hand pressed against a cut artery, keeping me alive. It had been a close call.

They must have put a sedative in the IV, because I have no recollection of my left wrist being handcuffed to the frame. I only found that out later when I tried to sit up. That was after I heard someone say the X-rays had been negative and the restraining straps removed.

It was just before noon when a green-clad doctor pronounced me okay to walk on my own, but told me my neck had been badly bruised and to be careful that my throat didn't swell closed. He wanted to admit me over night but I would have none of it.

It took another fifteen minutes before the police officer released the cuffs, but not before glaring at me for a long moment.

I started to walk to my car and then remembered why I had come here in the first place. I found the main desk and asked about Mark. His room had been changed to the third floor and his condition was now listed as stable. That was good news because it had been critical the last time I had checked.

I went up to his room and found him awake and talking quietly with his mother.

"How are you doing?" I managed to ask, my voice a horse whisper. I was happy to see him sitting up.

"They tell me the worst is over. The swelling has gone down, and if it doesn't return I'm going home in the morning."

"He looks good," Nora said, smiling broadly. "I'm so thrilled he's awake. He's a good boy, and I don't know what I'd do if he was gone."

"I'm not going anywhere, Mom. I'm okay."

"Where's Trich?" I asked. I had to talk to her and the sooner the better. She had a lot of explaining to do.

"She left this morning right after breakfast," Nora answered. "She was gone before they woke Mark up. I thought she was coming right back, but I was wrong."

"I tried to call her before, but no answer on her cell," Mark said. "I can't find my phone, and I think she has it." He turned to his mother. "I have something I need to discuss with Mr. Redstone, Mom. Can you wait outside? Only take a minute."

"If you insist. Not too long, mind you." She turned to me. "Don't keep him long. He needs to rest," she admonished, the mother taking over. She reluctantly stood and shuffled out of the room.

When she was gone, Mark said, "You know, being in a coma is strange. You know things and you don't know things. Voices float in and out. You don't actually hear the words, not all of them anyway, but you get senses. I knew when my mother was here, I could feel her at first. Then I could sense her voice. I imagine it's like being in heaven and knowing what's going on below." He reached for his water, sipped through the straw, and then continued. "When you folded my legs, it came to me what you were doing. I was happy you figured it out."

I felt my face getting warm. I thought I was beyond blushing, but I was sure color had appeared on my cheeks. "Did you," I began, "how should I ask this? Did you help it out?"

"I tried to, but didn't know if anything worked. Just like I tried to move my fingers when Mom was touching me. I can't tell if I did or not."

"How did you know I had it if you weren't sure it came out?"

"I figured it out, early this morning. I think it was early, but time is of no importance when you're in a coma, but everything was quiet, two voices came in the room. The sense of them was overpowering. I think because they were the same voices I heard just before I fell. Anyway, they had someone else, I think, a woman, but I'm not positive. Something cold was put on my skin and someone pressed it all over." He sipped some more water.

"Sonogram," I said, and he looked puzzled for a moment and then realized what I had said.

"Yes, something like that. Then they got all excited, and started talking faster than I could follow. I think I was waking up then, so I heard more, but still not everything. Heard your name mentioned and they were angry. When they left, I tried to hear if Trich was there but did not feel or see her."

"What else do you remember?"

"Not much. Nothing actually, until later I felt myself moving, floating really. I tried to open my eyes and couldn't. I still couldn't move my fingers. I faded in and out. Then, suddenly, I was awake, and two doctors were standing over me, and Mom was in the room."

"When was that?"

"I don't know. I guess about an hour or so ago. Maybe two. Don't know."

"I do have the flash drive," I told him. "Seems a lot of folks want it."

"It's in a water tight seal, so if you leave it there it'll be fine. The contents are government property so protect it."

"Its safe. At least for now."

"Have you seen it?"

"Not yet. Need a computer and I don't have mine."

"Protect that file at all costs. It has proof on it of who killed that man. I know the why. Look, don't bother looking at it. There's a code on it anyway, so you'll only see garbage. But even if you could, it won't mean anything to you. Someone would have to interpret it for you. Just protect it for me. It's my safety valve."

"Are you safe with that knowledge? They tried to kill you once."

"No. No. That was an accident. They were in my apartment, and I surprised them when I came in. One of the men grabbed me from behind, but he must have slipped and I got loose. I tried to get out but I tripped over a briefcase or something on the floor. I hit my head on a table."

"That was not exactly an accident."

"No, but they didn't try to knock me out or anything. They want the file."

"Who are they?" I asked, wondering if he even knew.

"Unless I miss my guess, and I think I'm right on this, they work for Homeland Security. Actually, they might even be Coast Guard."

"You got to be joking!" I actually knew Mark would never joke about the service he loved so much. He had to be on to something big.

"You know me better than that! Look, I don't pretend to know everything of what's going on, but this I do know. Captain Boyle was on the ship we approached. You remember he was on the radio? I thought he was talking from Corpus, but I checked the log books, a friend did me a favor, and the Captain was on the water that day. Log doesn't say where he was, but that adds up."

"That was a shrimp boat. What was he doing on a shrimp boat?"

"That's what I couldn't figure. I checked some records. As station commander, I have access to files others don't. Anyhow, remember the vessel had no name. It was one of ours that we use from time to time to intercept drugs. Those were our men on that ship. There's a secret mission underway. I could see some orders, but not all of it."

"Drugs?" I asked. "Is this about drugs? 'Cause if so, they already came in."

"At first I thought so. But from bits and pieces I pulled together I think it's bigger than that. Much bigger."

"What the hell can be bigger than interceding the drug traffic?"

"Terrorist activity. I think...no I'm certain, this is about smuggling terrorists into the country."

I remained silent, processing what Mark had just said. My bits and pieces matched his perfectly. An Asian rousted from his bed, a highly trained Asian at that, disappearing from the beach even though he was mostly naked, fit the puzzle. Maybe it wasn't a corner or edge piece, but it certainly had the right shades to belong in the mix. "But people are always coming across the borders. That's what the fence along the Rio Grande is about."

"Those are hit or miss Nationals, a few from other countries, mostly migrant workers seeking to make a few bucks, maybe have a baby here. Maybe some drug traffic. Not saying that's good or bad, but it's not what I'm talking about."

Again he sucked on the straw, his mouth was dry, and there were cracks in his lips. "Want me to get a nurse?" I asked.

"Not yet. In a bit. Anyway, what I'm talking about is a major plot to land about ten, maybe fifteen, highly dangerous men. They have a mission to destroy something big, really big, as a sign that we can't stop them."

"Any idea what that will be?"

"Guesses only. They're coming into the Midwest, so I assume the target is out here somewhere. I've thought of big targets in this part of the country, and the only thing that comes to mind is a dam. Hoover Dam, maybe. Is that too far fetched?"

"Not in the least. Certainly would make a statement."

"Then I had the thought, why so many men? Maybe they plan to bring down several dams at the same time. What is that one up on the Columbia River? My mind's still a bit fuzzy."

"Grand Coolie. Biggest hydroelectric producer in the country. Second or third in the world. They pull that off, we're in a world of hurt."

"Can I come back now?" Nora asked from behind me.

Not waiting for me to answer, she walked over to the bed and took his hand. "My God, look at him. Jimmy you got to go now, you have him all worked up. He needs to rest. I need him to get well."

"Mom, I'm okay. Going to be just fine."

"Nonsense! A mother knows what's best. Mr. Redstone can come back later on when you've rested. Can't you, Jimmy?"

"That will be just fine. I have work to do. By the way, does Trich know who I work for?"

"She might have guessed, but I never told her. Just that you were a friend of Pops."

"Please keep it that way."

"Why? Is there a problem?"

I debated what to say. I was beginning to have my suspicions, but nothing concrete. "No, just that I'm working low key down here, and the less who know the better."

"Okay. I'll not say anything."

I hugged Nora on the way out, and she said, "I heard you talking about Patricia. She's a very nice young woman. Did you know she's a nurse? Mark needs to get well, so he can get married. We're already planning the wedding."

TWENTY-THREE

This was the second time in two days my car had been searched. Now I was happy I hadn't spent a lot of time cleaning it after the episode at the dunes. Whoever tossed it this time had made no pretext of being subtle. The contents of the glove box were on the front seat, and the floor mat from the trunk was on the back floor along with the tire changing tool. A few hats and an old blanket were piled on top. The spare tire was laying inside the trunk out of its well. These guys were determined to find that flash drive and, until they did, it was going to be open season on me and my possessions. I had received their message loud and clear.

I checked my cell phone and found it switched off. While it sought out its orientation, I put the tire back in the well and dumped the stuff from the backseat into the trunk. Not bad considering all the damage these guys could have left behind.

How many were there? Two in the room, one working the car, perhaps a fourth standing guard. They had known the drive was not in the car so they were in radio contact. My guess, four, five at most.

Mark's supposition was most likely right on that whoever had tossed his place was working for the government. That's who called 911 when Mark was injured. That's why my gun was left behind, minus ammunition. Most importantly, that's why I hadn't received a parting kick. Professional courtesy—at least what passes for it with these thugs.

They now knew I was on their side—at least working for the Government. That would slow them down somewhat. I was sure their tactics would now change. One Ranger had already died; they were not going to chance another on their watch. It would raise too many political questions, and political questions were exactly what this bunch dreaded.

The cell phone chirped, indicating a message had been received sometime ago. Actually, four text messages, three from Angella, one from Trich:

Martinez 9:10AM Checked condo. Nothing conclusive.

Martinez 11:30AM: Tried to call. Where are you?

Martinez 12:45 PM: Called Mark. Room's changed. Mother says he's sleeping. You just left. What's going on?

Santiago: 12:15PM: I tried to call you earlier. My phone was missing but its back now. So is Mark's. A puzzle. I went home to change and fell asleep. Be back to see Mark about 2:00.

It was now almost one PM. I dialed Angella's number. She answered on the first ring. "Listen, don't talk. I'll clear this with Duran, but get here to the hospital, Brownsville, by one-forty five. We're going to interview Trich in depth; If we don't like her answers, we'll arrest her. I'll explain later. Need to coordinate with the locals. That's Duran's job. I'll get a bite to eat, if I can. My throat is swelling, hard to swallow. Had a go round with some guys who wanted the file. More later. They took my ammunition, all of it." I told her what I needed and she had extra. No problem.

Duran, as before, listened to my account of what happened, and then simply said, "I'll set it up with Brownsville. Could use State Police for this but politically, locals are better. The hospital's involved and those people are trained for that. Eat in the hospital lunchroom and someone will be along in a few minutes. Brief them directly. Angella will have to haul ass to get there in time."

Next call was to my boss, Lt. Contentus. As Duran had done, he listened silently and, when I finished, said, "That squares with what we've picked up. The hydroelectric stuff is new to me, but the security levels have been increased in the mid-west. Don't know if they extend to Nevada and the Northwest, but I'll check. And Jimmy, get it right with the girl. I know she's Mark's fiancé, but don't cut her slack. Do what you need to do. A lot hangs on this—a lot."

We both knew I didn't need that warning, but bosses are bosses, and he was protecting his skin in case I made a foolish mistake.

I had barely hung up from Contentus when two uniformed officers from the Brownsville Police came through the doors of the cafeteria. I placed a bowl of vegetable soup on my tray. I didn't trust my throat to work properly, so I limited my intake to mostly fluids. It was sore and could swell closed with not much encouragement. I recognized the smaller of the two as the one who had removed the cuffs in the emergency room. The man of no words.

He came over and said, "Wait for you over there. Boss'll join us in a few minutes. This must be big."

I nodded and continued through the line. When I took my seat, his partner introduced himself as Sergeant Sanchez and nodded toward his partner, Patrolman Guerro. They wore the uniform of the Brownsville Police Department. Guerro said, "You're the guy refused to answer my questions, should'a arrested you. Texas Ranger or no Texas Ranger. Should'a checked in with us."

"Sorry, I was drugged then. Someone gave me a sedative before the X-ray and I wasn't thinking straight."

"I bet," Guerro responded. "Carrying a gun in the hospital was enough reason to arrest you."

Sanchez put his hand up. "We don't need to be getting into it with Ranger Redstone. He screwed up, he paid the price." He turned to me. "Mind telling us what gives? You want our help, we have to know what's going down. Don't get much call for saving Ranger's down this way. Mostly drug shit going on. This hospital is right in the thick of it. This to do with drugs?"

I stalled just long enough for their commanding officer, Lt. Raymond Ortega, to join us. He came through the door of the cafeteria, and both men stood. He was a large man with a pleasant face. Hard eyes. He motioned the patrolmen back into their chairs.

Without preamble, he began, "Chief Duran filled me in. This Santiago woman, is she likely to present a threat? Do we need backup?"

"I doubt it, but the woman does work here, so she knows her way around. She has friends in case she decides to bolt. Other than that possibility, I don't make her as dangerous."

"Why the possible arrest?"

"I can't tell you much more than Duran already did because a lot of what's going on is confidential, need to know basis. Sorry about that. But a major drug deal's going down and she may be the local eyes. Her father is the Mexican headman for a part of the operation.

"Yes, that's Roberto Alterez Santiago," Ortega responded. "Know him well. More accurately, know of him. Seems no one really knows him. He could be sitting having lunch over there for all we know. No one has his picture. Rumor has it he spends time in the States, most likely comes across under an assumed name and ID. Occupation is listed as importer-exporter. Imports used cars and exports tomatoes and avocados." The lower part of his face smiled a knowing smile. His eyes remained cold and penetrating.

Ortega was impossible to read.

"That's his official occupation. Unofficially, we know he actually exports cocaine."

"What about illegals? Any history of aiding and abetting illegals into the Country?"

"Not that we can document. But wouldn't be a bit surprised. You got something on him along those lines, I'd be interested in hearing about it."

"Just wondering out loud. You got anything on his daughter? I've checked immigration and she's clean. Been coming across the bridge daily for over five years."

"She's clean from all we hear. We've watched her off and on, trying to see if we could match her up with her father. But the only person we ever see her with is the guy in the Coast Guard. The one I understand is here in the hospital."

"It's possible she's feeding her family information on the Coast Guard station. The station seems to be involved in this drug deal, and the burning question, of course, is what role Miss Santiago has and is playing. That's what I'm here to find out. I'm expecting my partner, a lady uniform on temporary assignment from the Island, any minute now."

Lt. Ortega consulted his notes, pulled out his radio, said a few words, listened, and reported, "Officer Martinez is a block away. She's being escorted."

"Thanks, didn't need to do that."

"Wouldn't want her to get a speeding ticket, now would we?" He smiled again, this time his eyes softened. "And by the way, thanks for including us in the operation. Doesn't happen that way all the time. You're Rangers. Could have used your own. We'll repay the favor when we get a chance."

"Thanks. Hope I never have to ask." And I meant that. "Can one of your officers arrange a room for us to talk with Trich, Miss Santiago? I want it to seem spontaneous."

"Best place is right here," Ortega suggested. "You didn't touch your soup. Just invite her to sit with you while you eat, tends to put people off guard. Breaking bread and all that."

I checked my watch and it was almost two. I sent a text to Trich: **How about joining me for a quick bite before we go up and see Mark? Have some news for you. Waiting in the lunchroom.**

Her answer came back almost immediately: **See you in a minute.**

I repeated her reply across the table and all three men stood and started out of the cafeteria. "We won't be far if you need us," Sergeant Sanchez responded.

I motioned Ortega back to the table. I held up my cell phone and cycled back through a few pictures until I found the one I wanted. "If this man shows up, he's trouble. They work in pairs, maybe two pairs. Run them out of the hospital would you?"

"Text that picture to me. I'll pass it along." He gave me his cell number and followed his men into the hall.

I entered his phone number and clicked SEND.

Finished just as Trich walked in. No sooner had she sat down but Angella appeared in the doorway, unsure whether to approach or not. I called to her, "Hey, Angella, over here. Having a bite to eat. Get something and join us. Trich, you hungry at all?"

"I could use a cold drink. It's hot out there."

"Name it."

"Diet Sprite."

I went over to Angella and asked her to pick up two diet Sprites and some bread. She looked at me with a strange expression, but said nothing.

"I already got the soup, case you're wondering," I said to her.

"You're throat is swollen. Looks like hell. You sure you're okay to do this?"

"No, I'm not sure. But what's the alternative?"

Back at the table, I said to Trich, who was wiping moisture from her face, "Angella will bring your drink over." I studied her a moment, not wanting to get too far into this without Angella being present. If for nothing else, I'd need confirmation of everything Trich said, as well as everything we said if any charges were to stick.

Trich ran her fingers through her hair and began to fidget in her seat. The silence had grown too long, so I said, "Did you hear Mark's awake?"

"When I found my phone I called him immediately. We had a nice chat until his mother cut him off. She's a protective one she is. Like my mother, always worrying about her family."

"All she has left is Mark, can't blame her," I responded, as Angella approached with a tray. When she was seated, I turned to Trich. "You said Nora was like your Mom. In what way is that so?"

"You know, protective. Always worrying when I go out, what I'm doing, that sort of thing."

"She have any reason? I mean, you never get in trouble, right, so she has nothing to worry about."

"Not me, no."

"Who then? I mean do you have brothers that give her a fit? My mother never worried about me, but my brother was another story."

She fidgeted in her chair and took a long drink of soda. Her lips moved, but words did not form. Then, as if making up her mind, she said, "My two brothers were always in trouble. My father sent them away to school, and even that didn't work."

"What does your father do?"

"He's an exporter."

"Of what? What does he export?"

"Vegetables. Mostly tomatoes, sometimes avocados."

"You ever help him?"

"He would not allow it. Every time I asked, he would get angry. 'Women in my family don't work!' he lectured over and over. He told me over and over that it was a man's job to support his family, and if I worked it would be an insult to him. He was not happy when I came here to work. At least I was not working in Mexico where his friends could see."

"But you're still working. I don't understand."

"The new way. Outside of Mexico, he looks the other way. He is not happy I come here every day, but he does not stop me. I tell him it will help him if he gets sick. There will be a place for him at the hospital. Still he does not understand why this is important to me. My mother tells him to let me be. He listens to her. Only to her and no one else."

"That man I saw you talking with yesterday, you know, the one who I asked you about at the airport, do you know him?"

"No. But I've seen him several times."

"Have you had other conversations with him?"

"He asked me about Mark, also about that sonogram we did." She threw her hands to her face. "Oh, was that wrong for me to tell him about the sonogram?"

"Who do you think he is?" I asked, not answering her question.

"I don't know. He spooks me. I think he works for my father, spying on me."

"Why do you say that?"

"I think he's the one who took my cell phone—and Mark's. He's telling my father who I call, who I see! It disappeared when he was around. It came back after I saw him. He spooks me!"

"Has Mark ever met your family?"

"No."

"Does your family know you are engaged to Mark?"

Again she fidgeted and, this time, her face turned bright red. She looked down as if the floor held the right answer. "My father would not allow me to marry a Gringo. He hates Americans. My mother knows and that is why she's afraid for me."

"Have you told Mark all this?"

"He knows how my father feels. But he says he can't go visit my family anyway without approval since he is an officer. I don't understand Mark sometimes."

"Has anyone in your family asked you about what Mark does?"

She continued to study the floor and then, without looking up, replied, "My brother keeps asking me. Wants me to tell him everything about what Mark does, what time he goes to work, what shifts he's on, everything he says."

"And what do you tell him?"

"At first, I answered his questions. I thought he was just being interested in me and my life. But when he continued to ask questions to find out things about Mark, the boats they use, how many people work for him, that kind of stuff, I stopped telling him. That made him mad."

"He wanted to know about boats?"

"More even. Things like, how many boats do they have? The names of the men in charge of the boats. How many boats were out of service, that sort of stuff."

"And did you pass any of this along to your brother?"

"No, I did not. I would never do anything to harm Mark. I love him more than anything." Her eyes filled with tears and had turned red.

"Did you give any information about Mark, the Coast Guard Station, or me to anyone at all in the last few days"

She looked directly at me for the first time since we began the discussion. Then she looked at Angella. "What is she doing here? What's going on here? Who is she?"

"Angella Martinez, my friend."

"You are not being honest with me. I'm in trouble, aren't I? You sound like you are the police. Oh, dear!" She wiped her eyes, "Like Mark's father was. You were a friend of his father, so I think you work for the police also. Is that true?"

"Yes, Trich, I work for the State of Texas. Angella works for the South Padre Island Police Department."

"I'm in trouble, isn't that so? I've done nothing wrong. I love him! Is that a crime? To be in love with a man can not be a crime!"

"Mark has information someone wants. We want to be sure you're not part of passing that information along."

"Part of hurting Mark! How can you say that? I love him! We are to be married. How can I possibly want to hurt Mark? You are mistaken." Tears ran freely down her cheeks, and her eyes were now totally red. She didn't even attempt to dry them.

I backed off a bit, my tone less demanding. "You may be doing so without your knowledge."

"You are mistaken! I love him. I don't understand what is going on! Please tell me what is it you want from me. I did nothing wrong. Are you going to arrest me?" Her eyes darted from me to Angella and back to me. "You are, aren't you? You're going to arrest me. I did nothing wrong!"

I had more to ask her, and I didn't want her to stop talking. I changed the subject away from her. "Tell me about your brother. Does he work for your father?"

"I don't know anything about what my father does! He won't permit it. He sells tomatoes and avocados, that's what I know."

"So you don't know if he's involved with Cocaine and other drugs?"

She threw her hands up to cover her face. Her shoulders shook for so long that I finally put my arms around her and pulled her close.

Angella frowned at my action. But I couldn't do otherwise. Either Trich was the best actress I had ever seen, or she was a woman clearly in distress. I put my money on the latter.

"Tell me he's not in drugs," she pleaded. "Please tell me that. I couldn't stand to think my father causes the ruined lives I see come into this hospital day in and day out. I see what the drugs do, and I can't bear to know my own father is the cause of this destruction."

"I'm afraid he is, Trich. I'm afraid so."

"Oh, my God!" she cried. "They won't let Mark marry me! Not if my father is doing what you say! I don't believe you're right about him. My father is a good man. He won't hurt anybody."

"Who won't allow that? Who are you talking about?"

"The US Government. How can a drug dealer's daughter marry an officer in the Coast Guard? They won't allow it!" She buried her face in her hands and her body again began to shake uncontrollably.

"I believe you may be wrong about that, Trich. The United States is not that way." Even as I was saying it, I knew she was probably right. If the Coast Guard brass determined Mark's wife was a threat, his career would be over.

I felt sorry for both of them, but I wasn't here as the Chaplain. My job description was to find criminals and arrest them. More particularly, I was focused on solving two murders and not worrying about the life of a love-struck child. "Trich, I want you to pull yourself together and tell Angella and me the truth and the full truth now. You understand? This is your chance to save your life with Mark. Tell us what you know. And be honest. Will you do that?"

"Yes," came the muffled response, "I love him. I will tell you what I know. But I did nothing wrong. Her face was still covered, her head bent almost between her legs. I thought she was about to throw up.

"Now please sit up and talk to us. This is important."

It took over a minute, but she managed to bring her shaking under control and finally she sat up straight. She pulled a tissue from her bag and dried her eyes.

When she was composed, I asked, "Are you prepared to tell us everything and to be truthful about it?"

"Yes."

"In the United States, you are always entitled to a lawyer to be present. Do you want a lawyer?"

"No. I did nothing wrong. I don't need a lawyer."

"If you can't afford a lawyer then one will be provided. Do you understand?"

"I understand. I have nothing to hide. I don't need a lawyer. I don't want one."

"Okay, Officer Martinez will record everything we say here, is that okay?"

"I have nothing to hide. I did nothing wrong."

"I need for you to answer the question. Is it okay for us to record this conversation?"

"Yes," came the muffled response. "Yes, do what you want. I love him."

For the next hour and a half, I stepped through her relationship with Mark and how she met him, her relationship with her father, with her brothers, and even with her mother. We discussed the man who she claimed removed her cell phone. She answered every question without hesitation, fighting back tears as she went.

When it was over, it was clear we did not have enough evidence to arrest her. She might have been guilty of spying on the Armed Forces, but most of the information she had passed along was publicly available from any number of sources. The FBI would have to sort through the transcript to determine if she or Mark had committed any Federal crimes. We were here for a murder investigation and a terrorist invasion, and she certainly knew nothing of the murders and essentially nothing about smuggling illegals into the country. Holding her on suspicion of espionage would serve no purpose and, in fact, would be a distraction.

When we were finished, I said, "Trich, I'm sorry to put you through this, but it's vital that we get to the bottom of what's going on. Please be careful what information you pass on to anyone concerning Mark and the Coast Guard. If anyone asks you anything, anything at all along those lines, please immediately let me or Officer Martinez know. It's important."

"Am I in trouble? I love Mark. I want to be married to him. We want to be together."

"As far as I know you're okay. But keep your nose clean."

Puzzled, she reached for her nose and asked, "What about my nose?"

"Just don't pass on any information about Mark, that's all. And please don't tell anyone about this interview. That's important."

"I promise," she replied.

I only hoped it was not already too late.

TWENTY-FOUR

On the drive back to the Island I mentally debriefed our interview. It kept me from focusing on the work I still had to do to make my car presentable. It also kept my mind from dwelling on my throat, which hadn't swollen closed but still burned with each breath of air.

During the interview, Angella had followed up on several questions, even asking if Trich happened to have a picture of her brother, Alverez Santiago, on her cell phone. When Trich obediently pulled up a picture, Angella studied it as if looking at a friend's new baby pictures and then, smiling, she said, "Would you text that to me?" Trich hadn't known what to do. Her inclination was to not do so, but she was desperate to please us, to avoid losing her lover. In the end, she relented and sent the picture to Angella.

Out of the corner of my eye, I had watched as Angella immediately relayed the picture to someone on SPI. My guess was it had gone directly to Chief Duran himself. Throughout the interview, as a name would surface, she would immediately forward it to SPI for background checking. She was obviously receiving live feedback because she would ask follow-on questions, clarifying a point here and there. The questions she asked were calculated to test the truthfulness of the information. I had never before taken part in an interrogation where people in a remote location were pulling the strings.

As the interview was winding down, Angella asked, "When did you see your brother Alverez last?" Making the question sound like natural conversation, one person interested in another.

"Don't recall," Trich had replied. "Not for a while."

"A week? Two weeks? A month?" Angella pressed.

"I really don't remember?"

"Was he home for Mother's day?"

"Yes, no wait. He came home the night before. That's always been our special time with Mother."

"So the end of May?"

"No. No. In Mexico Mother's Day is on May tenth. Always May tenth."

"So he was there, you say, May ninth. That the last time you saw him?"

"I don't recall any other time since, but he might have been around since then."

"Think hard, this is important," Angella continued to lean into Trich. The woman was a natural interrogator.

"Maybe once, possibly twice. Could be more."

"When was the last time he pestered you for information?"

"A few days ago."

"I thought you haven't seen him for weeks?"

"He called."

"Called? When was that?"

"Don't remember, exactly."

"Was it before Sunday?"

"Yes, maybe Saturday. No, not Saturday. Maybe Friday."

"Was it Friday?"

"I think so."

"Morning or night?"

"After work. It was Friday?"

"What did he ask you?"

"When I was going to see Mark."

"What did you answer?"

"I don't know. I answered, I don't know."

"What did your brother say?"

"He wanted me to be precise. Said it was important. Asked if I'd be seeing Mark on Sunday? I said, yes, for church."

"What did he say?"

"Then he's not working Sunday. That's what he said. He's not on shift on Sunday."

"I told him we were going to church, so Mark was not scheduled to work."

"Did he say anything else?"

"Nothing else."

"And that was the last time you two spoke?"

"Yes."

"You're positive?"

"Yes, I'm sure."

"Where did he call from?"

"Don't know?"

"US or Mexico?"

"I don't know."

Later, when I commented to Angella that she had done a superb job at the interview, she thanked me and then responded by commenting on how everybody involved in this mess knew everyone else. One great big grab bag. Trich's father and brother involved in drugs; Trich dating the head of the Coast Guard drug interdiction apparatus; Homeland Security people following us; the list went on.

When I asked Angella to again give me her opinion on Trich, without hesitation, she replied, "If you're asking me if she's involved in drug trafficking, I'd say, not directly. Do I think her family is using her? You bet your bullets I do. Big time. I also think her brother knew something was going down on Sunday and was concerned where Mark would be. Maybe to work around him or just maybe to keep him out of harm's way. I'll bet he's into this up to his eyeballs. I'll even bet her brother's on the Island."

"No takers here," I had replied. "You're right on."

My thoughts lingered on Angella. She was remarkable for a rookie detective and, from what I could see, was a natural. I wouldn't at all mind having her as my partner, but that would mean I'd have to forego fantasizing about her as a woman. I wasn't sure I wanted to go that far.

The last time around I ended up losing both my partner and my marriage. This time, there was no marriage to contend with, but romantic attachments lead to bad field decisions and, ultimately, someone is injured or worse. They are simply not good. Contentus had made that clear enough the last time around.

The fact remained, however, that Angella, from everything I knew about her—and admittedly that was not very exhaustive— was someone I knew I could easily become involved with. The problem for me has never been could I fall in love. The question has always been, how long I would remain in love.

Thinking of Angella, I even began to believe I could not only fall in love but, given half a chance, I could remain in love with her for a very long time. She had the attributes I admired. And the physical attraction was an added plus.

The only question I harbored now was whether the feeling was mutual.

TWENTY-FIVE

It was four-thirty when I crossed the bridge and turned north onto Padre Boulevard, the main street that runs right up the center of the Island about fifteen or so miles. There are only two other north/south streets, and they only extend a few miles. Gulf Blvd runs parallel and to the east of Padre Boulevard along the Gulf of Mexico. Laguna Boulevard runs parallel to the west, along Laguna Madre, the body of water separating SPI from Port Isabel and the rest of Texas.

Padre Boulevard continues north to where it ends in a sand dune. As I found out when I went camping with Angella, the beach runs about twenty-five miles north, and the only way to get there is by a vehicle capable of running on sand.

This stretch of earth must be a nightmare to patrol. I wonder what stopped drug runners from picking up their cargo along the Gulf surf where we camped and taking it across the spit of sand by ATV and crossing Laguna Madre by boat.

If I figured this out, so had the drug runners and, therefore, so had the rest of law enforcement. What they were doing about it,

I had no way of knowing at the moment. I made a mental note to get the answers. My immediate thought was they had this under air and satellite surveillance, but even then, the information would be hours too late. Something more must be in place.

And that's where Paco fit in for the bad guys. He specialized in retrieving cargo from the waters of the Gulf of Mexico and delivering it safely inland. A sophisticated operation resulting in a colossal game of cat and mouse. From what I had observed so far, the mouse was winning.

I caught up to Angella in the parking lot of Joy's condo. She was leaning against her car, squinting at the screen of her cell phone, trying to read a message.

When I approached, she said, "Good news for a change. Got a match! James Alterez and Alterez Santiago are one in the same. And get this. Chief Duran put Alterez's picture out on the Valley Network and we hit pay dirt. Port Isabel got a match. Seems our friend James is known on that side of the lagoon as Jay. Jay Alterez applied for a fishing license and rented a motorboat. Busy little beaver. Man got more drivers licenses than I got shoes."

"Hold on a minute! Your boat's moving but there's no one at the helm!"

"What the hell you mumbling about now?"

"Sorry, can't get the words out just right, throat's sore as hell. I catch that son of a bitch, I'll shove his head –"

"Save your voice! I can't understand you anyway."

"Oh, shit. Start at the beginning. I don't know who you're talking about. James Alterez is who now?"

"I went to interview the apartment owner earlier when you went off to Brownsville. Man wasn't there." She nodded toward the building. "As you can see, it's a six-floor condo, owner leased, so there's no front desk. I checked with the maintenance chief, an old guy, barely able to walk, drags his right leg, but he knows what's going on. Told me the tenant checked out the day they found Heart."

"What's the tenant's name. Let's start there."

"Actually, I was just getting there. You always this impatient? You're going to find this interesting. Guy's name is James Alterez. Rented the condo for the summer. Supposed to have a job at *Paragraphs*, the bookstore. Dead end. Never heard of him there."

"Have you contacted the condo owner? Get more info on this guy?

"Been trying. The man travels, almost never here. The old guy said he's in Kyoto or someplace in Japan. Owner seems clean, no record, no incidents. Just a guy with more money than he knows what to do with, so he travels. We're running it though." She went silent for a moment, then said, "I was about to tell you something and the thought slipped away. Give me a moment and it'll come back."

"You said I would find something interesting."

"Oh, yea. The name Alterez, James Alterez. The guy who skipped out. Trich's brother's name is Alterez. That seems to be a family name."

"Have you shown the picture to the old guy. Bet we have a match."

"I just got here a moment before you. Haven't had a chance yet."

"It's time we visit Joy. Lean on her a bit, see what joy she brings us."

Angella smiled at my silly play on words. "On the way up, let's find the old guy and try on the picture. Give us more to go on with Joy."

Before we even took two steps both our cell phones came alive.

There was no doubt about the message from Captain Duran. **Both of you report to my office immediately!**

Be there in five, Angella replied. I fell into her car and we traveled the five blocks in silence.

Duran didn't bother with pleasantries. "Now tell me what the hell's going on!" Duran had addressed me, but it was clear he was holding Angella accountable as well. "Coast Guard, in the form of Captain Boyle, is all over my butt! Some fancy-ass take no prisoners General running this operation from Washington is all over him, got everyone stirred up. Governor's called ten times! Redstone, you apparently have video files that belong to the Coast Guard! They want your ass! What I want, I want the whole friggin' story! And I want it straight! We had an understanding on this and seems you don't give a shit about understandings!"

I tried to keep my voice calm, knowing that, if I got angry, it would be even worse for me. "The Coast Guard has taken to video taping certain situations in their boats. Mark found a video with some hard evidence on it, says the file shows how the body got on the beach. He copied the file from the boat computer to a flash drive. It's government property so he couldn't just walk around with it. He was afraid of leaving it at the station because, and I have to assume here, because it implicates the Coast Guard and maybe even Boyle. So he swallowed it. That's what they were looking for when he walked into his apartment and surprised them, the drive."

"You telling me the Coast Guard broke in to his place and that's who hit him on the head?"

"That's my guess. Mark says he fell, but he's covering for them. That's what I was mugged for on the beach. That file. I didn't have it then. I guessed what Mark had done and had a sonogram performed while he was in the coma. I retrieved the files. That's what they were looking for in my room."

"You telling me that's why you were jumped at the hospital. Since when don't you report criminal activity? Assault and battery.

Brownsville says you refused to discuss it with them. They're miffed to say the least. Had to cash in good will to get you out of that mess. You owe me."

"I was on a stretcher on my way to have my neck X-rayed. When they released me they didn't ask. I needed to find Mark and talk to him. In case you're interested, he's awake and doing well."

"Save the bullshit! You wanted to tell them, you would have told them! You Rangers got to play everything close don't you? It's in your friggin' blood! You telling me the Guard's doing all this? I don't believe it! Mark's been suspended from active duty. He's not done himself any favors in all this playing hide the muffin. Now they're calling for your ass! I'm in the middle and getting my ass chewed no matter which way I face."

"Not surprising about Mark. Actually he told me he automatically went on sick leave when he was admitted to the hospital, so it's moot for the moment. But I don't doubt they want him out of the way, at least for a while. He knows too much and until they get that file he's safe."

"They're going to court-martial him for disobeying orders. That's how they deal with folks who don't play ball. Sometimes I wish I had that option. Put a few of you in the brig, straighten you all out!" He looked directly at me, his eyes on fire, his chin set hard. "Too bad we don't have court-martial capability for officer's who don't do what they're told to do. Maybe a hanging or two would get through to you mavericks."

I tried to ignore the taunts; no good would come of it if Duran and I got in to it. "Not so easy to court-martial Mark. His record is clean, and he didn't violate any order. He maintained the file confidential. They, their thugs, are the ones who caused the file to be, shall we say, expelled."

"How long have you had that file?"

"Since late yesterday."

"And why haven't you reported it to me?"

"Because, Sir, with all due respect, you'd be obligated to give it to the Coast Guard. If there's evidence of civil wrong doing on that video it'll be lost. Didn't want to put you in that position."

"And you're prepared to put you career, and, as it turns out, your life, in jeopardy to protect what? Your sense of what's right and wrong! For all you really know, that file may be critically important to stopping the infiltration of terrorists. No, don't interrupt, I'm not finished! You think you're smarter than the rest of us. Texas Ranger and all that bullshit! We're just local yokels to you! You think we can't get out of our own headlights! I'm sick and tired of the friggin' games you folks play. I know good and well what's going down. There're terrorists being smuggled in, probably tonight or tomorrow night, and they're using the drug folks to handle the landside of it. We've known that for several days now. Don't need no desk-bound fancy-pants General sitting in a bunker deep under Washington, DC, telling me that. Then you come along on your white horse and what have you added? You got us cross-wise with Homeland Security! That's what! I gotta work with them when this is over, so now I have to go kiss their butts—and all because you didn't see fit to give me the file!"

He stopped yelling, but I knew he wasn't finished, so I held my tongue—and my temper. For all I knew, he was playing to the house. Maybe someone was listening to this tirade, or taping it. He had conveniently overlooked that it was my efforts, combined with Angella's instincts, that led us to the naked guy on the beach, and to Trich's brother and to his boat in Port Isabel, not to mention that we now knew who lived at the house where the second murder occurred. Not bad for a one-armed detective working with a virgin detective.

Something else was wrong here. There was too much emphasis on the video. If the Coast Guard had done nothing improper then why go to the lengths they have to retrieve the file? No, this was far from over.

I finally broke my silence. "I acknowledge I should have told you about the video, but truth is, who the hell knows why it's so important. If this was a matter of national security, you'd think they would have confided in you, especially if the video tells us who killed Nelson and how. Instead, they nearly broke my neck, tossed my room, and put Mark in the hospital. And you're worried about kissing up to them! They're not Boy Scouts on this either."

"Smart men can rationalize anything. That's why you guys go off half-cocked so often." He spun around to face Angella, who had been making herself as invisible as she could, without actually hiding under the table. "And as for you, young lady, when did you know he had the video?"

I tried to signal to her that it was okay to lie, but she never looked my way. "Soon after he retrieved the file I was pretty certain he had it," she responded, without a trace of concern for herself.

"And you didn't report it either?"

"No, Sir, I did not."

"You know what insubordination means?"

"Yes, Sir, I do."

"So why did you withhold the file?"

"Sir, I'm sorry for not coming forward. But, Sir, I was honoring my partner's decision."

Duran glared at Angella. It is difficult to discipline a person who is forthright in what she has done and for the right reason. Trust between partners is paramount to the efficient operation of a police force. They have each other's backs in situations where no one ever wants to be. Without absolute trust, cops would never be able to do what they are paid to do.

And Duran knew that as well as anybody knew it.

"I'll deal with you later, young woman," he said to Angella, "but don't ever let that happen again! Now both of you get back out there and solve this mess. And if either of you two withhold even a thought from me, I'll have your hides—and your badges. You hear me, Redstone?"

"Yes, I hear you."

"You hear me Martinez?"

"Yes, I hear you," Angela replied, using the same tone I had.

On the way out, I resisted the temptation of throwing a mock salute. Duran most likely would have shot us both.

Back in the car, Angella said. "I never saw him act that way. I thought he'd have a heart attack."

"All a show. Don't know who the audience is, but we were puppets, dancing to his tune."

"How you figure?"

"Did he ever ask for the file? No. Did he pull my badge and gun? No. Did he send you back to traffic duty? No. He knows about the terrorist infiltration, even the time schedule. But did he alert us? No. But truth is, he knows we're onto something. But I caution you, we're now expendable. Something goes wrong and he washes his hands of us. You'll spend the rest of your time patrolling latrines. I'll be sent out to pasture."

"So, what do we do?"

"Just what we were doing, finding the pieces. It's done one piece at a time. Takes time, probably more time than we have. On TV this stuff all happens in an hour. Less, if you count commercials. Out here, it happens when it happens, years sometimes. And, unfortunately, all too often, all of the pieces are never found. The problem is life is complicated—and messy. The puzzles overlap. Sometimes you find pieces that fit in some other puzzle and you try to work them into yours. I think that's what we have here, overlapping puzzles. When that happens, they're tough, often impossible, to sort out."

TWENTY-SIX

We arrived back at Joy's condo and took the elevator to the sixth floor penthouse.

"Hey, I was just going out," Joy exclaimed, when she opened the door. She appeared rushed and her smile was forced. The door was blocking our view into the living room, and I had the distinct impression there was someone there she didn't want us to see. "Happy hour has arrived," she continued, "can't keep my friends waiting. This looks serious. Let's talk in the morning."

"There's no time like the present," I said. "How about inviting us in?" I flipped my ID at her. She didn't so much as blink.

"Three's a crowd," she winked. "Wouldn't mind if this was one on one, but I'm getting too old for a threesome."

Her winks were calculated to make me think there were advantages if I'd come back in the morning—and without Angella. At one time, Joy must have been a knockout, but time, and the south Texas sun, had not been kind to her.

"Are we coming in or shall we talk in the hall?" I responded, trying to keep my voice pleasant, but I allowed a sharp note to creep in. The time for games was long past.

"I'm late already. Have to wait 'till morning. Sorry."

"Let me level with you. This conversation is going to take place now. Either we do it in the comfort of your living room, or we do it at the station. But we *are* going to have the conversation."

"You have a warrant for my arrest?"

"No, just want to talk."

"I don't have to answer and I don't have to invite you in unless you have a warrant. I know my rights."

"Smart lady. But let me point out something you may have overlooked. You gave a false police report. You told the officer that James Alterez, the man who rented the condo downstairs, the one where you were having your, shall we call them, *afternoon socials,* was a school teacher and worked at a bookstore this summer. In fact, Mr. Alterez is a National, certainly not a teacher, and you knew that. Why you lied, I don't know, but it's enough for us to hold you for obstruction of justice. Maybe after we dig a bit deeper, it might turn out you had more to do with the death, murder as you called it, than you'd want us to know. We do that, you'll miss more than one happy hour."

"Murder!" she exclaimed. "What the hell you talking about? He was my friend! I would never have murdered him, or anybody."

"You want to talk about it here or go to the station and see what else we have?"

She glanced over her shoulder, hesitated, then said, "Shit, come on in. We'll talk here. You've already ruined happy hour."

We followed her into the condo unit, which overlooked the Gulf of Mexico. The room was comfortably furnished but not overly done, which I suspected was normal for a property so close to the water. She slid the balcony door open, and the sound of the surf formed a pleasant background for our conversation.

Since I had already told her she was a suspect in a murder investigation, it was only proper then to read her rights to her. There was no downside to doing so, and if we did get some good evidence, some smart lawyer couldn't have it excluded because of Miranda warning failures. As expected, she declined having a lawyer present. Never a smart move, whether or not you have something to conceal, but that was her problem, not mine. Had she done so, the interview would have ended.

"Let's begin," I said, my voice now conciliatory, "with Mr. Alterez. How well do you know him?"

"Obviously not well, since you say he's not a school teacher. I had no idea he was from Mexico. Doesn't look it."

I had the same impression when I first met Trich. I would never have thought her to be anything other than a dark-skinned American, except for her accent. "So, you thought he was a teacher?"

"Yes."

"Why?"

"Because he told me so."

"When?"

"When I first met him."

"When was that?"

She hesitated before answering. "When he moved in. Back in May."

"You didn't know him before then, is that what you're telling us?"

She hesitated. "That's what I'm saying."

"Did he speak with an accent?"

She hesitated again. "Not that I heard."

"You sure?"

"He spoke perfect English."

So does Trich, but with a slight accent. Okay, back to the time frame. "So, if I were to show you a picture of yourself with Mr. Alterez taken last year you would tell me what?"

"I'd tell you it was a phony! One of them shopped photos like when they put a man's face on a horse, that sort of thing. I didn't know him before this year."

"Before May of this year?"

"Yes, just before Memorial Day he moved in."

"And you didn't contact the owner of the condo to rent it for Mr. Alterez?"

"I did no such thing."

"Then how come he says you did?"

"He's confused if he thinks that."

"So he's confused. Confused with who?"

"I don't know, confused that's all."

"You know, Joy, that's easy to verify."

"He's in Japan, good luck."

"How do you know he's in Japan? You just happen to keep tabs on all your neighbors?"

"I happen to know him that's all."

"When did you see him last? When was he here last?"

"In January or February."

"Of this year?"

"Yes, this year."

"You saw him here in this building in January or February of this year?"

"That's what I said. Doesn't change if you repeat it."

"Just want to be sure we heard you right. No misunderstandings."

"You got it right."

That was the opening we needed. We knew from Angella's conversation with the old maintenance man that the owner of that condo hadn't been here for over a year. Angella was alert, sensing we were onto something.

I purposely redirected the conversation. We had what we wanted on that subject and would circle back later. "Tell me," I began the new line of questioning "about your relationship with the deceased Heart. Mr. Jayson Monroe Hardwick, to be exact. He stayed with James Alterez this summer."

"What do you want to know?"

"How did you meet him? When did you meet him? All that stuff."

She was forthcoming about Heart. She repeated what she had told me at lunch, and added, "I felt comfortable with him. He was younger than I, but that didn't bother him like it bothers some men."

"If I recall right, you and Heart used the Alterez condo for your *socials*. Did you ever see Mr. Alterez there?"

"Hardly ever. He worked during the day. I never—visited at night. Afternoon's only." She looked at Angella and winked. "Afternoon's are best." When Angella didn't respond, Joy said, "try it, you'll like it."

"And what did Mr. Alterez think about you two spending afternoons in his place?"

"He was letting Heart stay there, what should he care?"

"Alterez worked at the bookstore you say."

"I thought so."

"Ever see him go to work?"

"No."

"Ever see him come home?"

"No."

"So he came and went and you never saw him."

"I saw him a few times, but I don't know where he was going or coming from."

"Was it the beach? I mean was he wearing a bathing suit or work clothes?"

"Work clothes."

"What was he wearing when you saw him?"

"You know, a shirt, pants, what everybody wears in the valley."

"A dress shirt, like with a tie, what?"

"What does it matter? A shirt. No not one with a tie. No one wears a tie down here."

"Long pants or short?"

"Long, I think."

"Shoes. Boating shoes, sneakers, sandals, what?"

"I don't know! Not sandals. As I think of it, he was wearing jeans and heavy looking shoes, like on a ranch."

"So he wasn't dressed to go boating, fishing, that sort of thing."

"Not that I saw."

"Tell me about your husband. What does he do?"

That opened a tirade of remarks that came so fast it was hard to keep good notes. From the picture she painted, the man did nothing but bet on anything and everything. He was running through her money and she was concerned. That was why she was planning on leaving him. No, she had not yet consulted a lawyer, but she was going to.

Yes, he knew about her affair, actually affairs, as she pointed out. She was on a roll and volunteered names and times of several others. All over now, she announced, proud of her accomplishments. When she thought Angella was not looking she flashed me another wink.

When she was finished, I asked, "Do you use drugs, and I don't mean the prescription kind?"

"Hell no!"

"Cocaine?"

"You got to be kidding. You really think I'd do that?"

"As a matter of fact, Joy, I do. I've seen you high and, unless I'm mistaken, and I certainly can be, that was a cocaine high the other night, not alcohol."

"Alcohol is my choice for party time."

"I'm making you as a cocaine user. Maybe you drink a little alcohol when you're out to throw people off, but you're heavy into drugs. Fess up now."

"Get out of here! This discussion is over! You want to arrest me, you arrest me! Otherwise, I'm going out. Now get out of here now!"

I stood and Angella followed my lead. "Keep your nose clean, Joy. You're on the hairy edge. If nothing else, possession of cocaine is a felony."

"Get out of here now!"

"Does your husband know of your addiction?" I asked, continuing the pressure on her. Sometimes it worked. This was not one of the times though.

"Get the hell out of here!" she was near hysteria, and I motioned to Angella to move toward the front door. I was not yet ready to arrest her, but her drug habit tied her to Alterez tighter than she had admitted.

Joy was in this much deeper than I had at first thought.

Neither Angella nor I spoke until the elevator doors closed. Then Angela said, "So this is how it's done. Poke, poke, poke until something pops."

"The real trick is knowing where to poke."

"You pull that cocaine use out of thin air or what?"

"Observation at the bar. Actually, your observation. She was high, but not drinking all that much. Last night, she was high again, and then when her husband showed up, she walked out unimpaired. Either she's acting drunk or it's something else. Just wanted to see her reaction."

"Well?"

"She hides it well. When I brought up the subject did you see her hand immediately go to her nose, as if to be sure there was no telltale residue? She's a user all right. And not a cheap habit at that."

"I agree she knows Alterez. There was noticeable twisting and discomfort when you brought up his name. She knows more than she's saying."

"What else did you notice?"

"She opened the patio door as if to muffle the sound."

"She stole glances at the bedroom door the whole time we were there. My bet is there's someone in there. Most likely not her husband."

"Why the open patio door?"

"So our voices would carry into the bedroom to warn whoever was there not to come out. We had no warrant, so going in there could have caused a bit of a ruckus. May even have messed up a future arrest."

"Who you think was in there?"

"My guess, Trich's brother. Alterez James Santiago. Could be resupplying her."

"So why not bust him?"

"Couple of reasons. One, we had no warrant and no probable cause. I was hoping to see drug evidence, but got nothing. Most importantly, never knew a drug dealer without a loaded and cocked weapon. One or both of us would be on our way to the morgue right now if we had moved in that direction."

"Thanks."

"Just doing my job. And how do you know I was protecting you? Get someone out here to watch the condo. I want to know who's in there."

Within ten minutes, a police truck pulled up, and a guy wearing the outfit of a maintenance worker slid out of the passenger seat, carrying a broom. Angella went over to him, spoke briefly, and then returned to the car.

"Okay. He'll take pictures of anyone coming out of the condo. I told him to stay for two hours. Will that be long enough or do you want more?"

"That should do it. No, check that. Have him wait three hours. Have him text the pictures to you as he gets them."

While I waited for Angella, I thought about Joy and our conversation. I was convinced the key to what was going down centered around her, but it was not feeling exactly right. The lady did drugs, and her lover died of an overdose. Much too pat. I didn't like this one bit.

"All set," Angella exclaimed, when she climbed back in the car. "Where to now?"

"Let's go see what the canvas notes tell us about the interviews of the condo folks the day Heart died. That is, unless you have a better idea."

"I would love to put this all on a big board like House does on that TV show. Then maybe we can see what we're missing."

"I'll bet Duran has a board working, let's go see if he'll share. Be a good way to tell him about Joy. He'll get his wish. Keep the man in the loop."

TWENTY-SEVEN

"Heard you finally rousted the Malcom woman," Duran said when Angella caught up with him in the hall outside his office. He had calmed down in the hour and half that we were gone, and I sensed something new in his manner. "Get anything we can use?" he asked, almost as if he already knew what we were going to say.

"She's got some things to hide, that's clear. She's a user. Cocaine, unless I miss my guess. We think there was someone in her bedroom listening to the conversation. Should get a lead on that person soon. Joy lied about her involvement with Alterez. I make him for her supplier. Heart dies of an overdose, that ties in."

"Heard about that. Want a warrant for her arrest?"

"Not yet. String her. Let's let it play a bit. Alterez is the key here. Let's see what he'll do next. Besides, we don't have enough for a warrant."

"The only good thing with the Feds looking over our shoulder and the red alert, they can get us anything we want. It's what you might call open season. You name it, we'll get it. This is wartime, my friend. Civil liberties, kiss them goodbye."

"Frightening thought. I may complain about how hard it is to get a warrant, but the system works. Makes it tough for guys like me, but that's what I fight for, to keep it working."

"Save the rah rah speeches for the school kids on parents' show and tell day. You tell me what you need, we'll get it done. Things are centering around Alterez. We need to talk with him, and the sooner the better."

"Disagree. Respectfully, that is. Guy like him always believes he's being followed. If he's a low man on this, then following him won't get the job done. If he's the top gun, he'll give us the slip anyway. We got to do this from afar."

"Let me think on that for a moment." Duran continued to pace around his makeshift office, clearly troubled and trying not to show it. "I say we roust him. If our mission is to prevent a terrorist attack, then preventing the attack is a win for our side."

"Sounds like the same shit Captain Boyle was handing me. They get to you?"

"Just being practical. Looking at the big picture."

"The way I see it, the big picture is their problem, not mine and not yours. All we can do is perform our respective jobs. For me, that's running Nelson's killer to ground and that's what I intend to do. I'd think our desires would be lined up, 'cause like it or not, Nelson landed on your beach."

"I don't need a friggin' civics lesson from you! I know my responsibility. I say get him running, he'll mess up. You want to work on this case, you get him running. You understand me?"

"Loud and clear. But I doubt if you have the resources to find a killer working from a boat that never even touched this beach."

"You never mind about resources. Got the whole friggin' navy, or rather Coast Guard, out there, that's what I have. Smart guy like you must have figured that out by now. In case you haven't, this operation is bigger than you know."

"We can't deal with the big picture. I only know how to deal with facts. You give me a fact, I'll run it to ground. Those guys in the boats and planes think they can find terrorists and murderers, let them at it."

Duran's face was getting red again when Angella came to my rescue. "Chief, we're trying to run him down. Don't know exactly where he is right now, but we'll get on him when we get out of here. What we came back for is to see if you got a board or something with everything lined up. I mean all the bits and pieces of this put out like I see the doctors do on TV."

"This ain't no stupid TV show, damn it! But I do happen to have put together a computer spread sheet." He went to the table, pushed aside several files, fiddled with his keyboard and mouse, and then motioned us around the desk to view the screen. "It's nothing more than what's already in your head, but here's what we have."

Actually, he had several screens of information, with arrows pointing back and forth among them. Nothing on the screens surprised me, except that one of the boards was a picture of the Island with colored dots spread around. Two of the dots represented the bodies. Duran explained the others.

My attention was focused on the upper part of the island, miles north of the city limits. In fact, miles beyond the end of the paved roadway, there were blue and green dots scattered all around.

Duran noticed that I had focused on those dots. "This is highly sensitive what I'm about to tell you. Homeland Security has installed electronic sensors on the island. That's the blue dots. They sense any motorized vehicle moving in a quarter mile radius. I don't know how they work so don't ask. But I'm told that if an ATV, or any other motorized vehicle, passes within their radius they will emit an alarm."

"Why only a quarter mile? Ones we use go out about a half mile."

"I'm told it's the sand. Absorbs the vibration."

"What about the green ones?" I asked, curious at the formation.

"The green dots are sound sensors. They're not so sensitive and the target needs to pass almost right over the sensor."

"I see that there are no green ones along the beach."

"Can't get too close to the water or they won't work. I don't know if it's the salt or the surf noise. But anyone going up or down the beach can't get anywhere. They have to cross the island to get to the bay. That's where they get caught by the sensors. This system actually works. We've picked up over twenty million in drugs in the last year alone." He touched his finger to a point about twenty miles north of the city near Laguna Madre. "Here's where they cross. The sensor tells the County where the ATVs are, and when they get to the Lagoon, we're waiting."

"Sounds like easy pickings. Then how did the drugs dropped the other night get through?"

"That's just it, they didn't. Picked up right here." He moved his pointer about two miles north of where it last had been. There's an opening in the dunes here and DEA was waiting. Came in from the Lagoon when the Coast Guard notified them of the drop time. Picked it up from heat sensors from a scan plane."

I was impressed with the elaborate set up, and it was clear that the bad guys and the good guys were way ahead of me when it came to drug smuggling across the island.

"So, you see why I leave the drug interdiction to others," Chief Duran said. "But that still leaves us with two dead bodies. If I was a free man in all this, that's what I'd concentrate on. I'd want that solved, and the sooner the better. I got to answer to the Mayor, and the Aldermen are leaning all over him to wind this up. Tourists are concerned. When tourists are concerned, I get concerned. You understand how that works."

"Something to do with gravity and the flow direction of waste products."

"And you're even further down hill than I am. But with the Governor calling and that friggin' General running roughshod over everything we do, I'm afraid the murders will just have to wait. Need to roust Alterez, and do it sooner rather than later."

TWENTY-EIGHT

M ark called to tell me he was feeling better and would be released in the morning, providing he had a good night. He also informed me that they had posted a guard outside his door, and only the nurses and his mother were allowed in to see him. Trich had been turned away. "I don't know if I'm under arrest or what," Mark said. "Something's wrong at the station. One of my guys called and started to tell me, but stopped. I think someone was coming. They've been told not to talk to me."

"I'm sorry to hear that," I replied, trying to walk a middle line between cheering him up and giving him false hope.

"I know they'll pin it all on me! It's the end of my career. This is my life, the only life I know—or want!"

I tried to soft-talk it, hoping the issues would resolve, but knowing we were both fighting uphill battles. When the government is against you, the odds of winning personal battles are slim.

"Okay," I said when the conversation wound down, "let me know when you get back to your apartment and let me know if you need any help. I assume your mother is going to stay with you while you recuperate."

"That's her plan, but frankly, one day will be enough. I might need your help getting her to go home."

"Whatever I can do," I replied, not looking forward to tangling with Nora Cruses.

Captain Duran called to tell Angella and me that Immigration learned from the two men picked up in the raid that they had come into the country together. One Korean and four Columbians. Two of the Columbians were taken somewhere else; the inform- ant didn't know where. They were planning to meet up with them tomorrow and get further instructions then. Each of the men was proficient with weapons and skilled boaters. They were to be paid good money and they only knew their mission was going to be dan- gerous.

"How did they get in the country?"

"By boat. They were transferred at sea, but were blindfolded. Seems a dead end."

"Anything more? Did they overhear anything?"

"They speak very little English."

"But still, they must have heard something."

"If they did, INS isn't saying."

"Did they land in the water, on a beach, what?"

"All I was told is they were dry when they came ashore. I have to assume they landed on a dock of some sort. A fishing pier maybe."

"Any leads on the missing two?"

"Nothing yet. Oh, by the way, your friend Captain Boyle is looking to talk to you. The man's calmed a bit, but clearly still agi- tated. Wants you to call ASAP."

"We'll do better than that. Angella and I'll drop by to see him. Is he still running the radio at the Station?"

"That attitude won't get you far. But he's there."

"Good, it's time for a visit anyway."

"I can't protect you if you get your ass in a sling over there. You better hope you got a Rabbi or something in Austin 'cause Boyle may have calmed down, but he's still loaded for bear. He's got your boy Mark under house arrest and, unless I'm mistaken, he has you in his sights."

On the way to the Coast Guard station, my boss Contentus called. "Better get your ass over to see Boyle as fast as you can. He's looking for you. It doesn't sound like he's inviting you to play canasta."

"What the hell's going on?" I asked. "All of a sudden Boyle's running the show. What gives?"

"He'll brief you."

"Last time he and I spoke, he threatened to court-martial me. Am I safe going to the station?"

"He and I have an understanding on that. You behave, he allows you to leave."

"Big of him," I replied into a dead line.

Boyle had left word with the guard at the entrance not to disturb him except in case of emergency.

"Tell Captain Boyle it's an emergency," I said to the young man stationed at the front door.

"Sir, what is the nature of the emergency?"

"He'll have your ass for breakfast if he finds out we were here and you turned us away. That enough of an emergency for you, Son?"

"I have orders, Sir. And my discomfort is not sufficient to disturb him, Sir." The man held his ground, and I was proud of him for doing so.

"Listen, Son, lives are in danger. I've spoken with your commander, Lt Cruses, and he agrees this is an emergency."

"You've spoken to the Lieutenant? How's he doing?"

"Much better. I'll tell him you asked after him."

"We're all worried for him. He's a great guy, treats us right. I've served under a lotta men, and he's by far the best. If he says it's an emergency, then it must be. Stay here and I'll be back in a moment."

When the young man disappeared, Angella said, "Hope you didn't just get him busted."

"That's between him and Boyle, I'm afraid. Boyle asked for us; you'd think our names would be at the front desk, so to speak."

He was gone less than a minute. "Sir, the Captain will see you now," he said on his return. "Tell the Lieutenant Seaman Oliver sends his regards. Captain is down the hall, second left."

Boyle was wearing blue trousers and a blue shirt. On his shoulder bars there was a gold medallion and four wide bars. I wasn't certain of their meaning but my guess was that four of anything was a fairly high ranking.

He was sitting on a wood chair at the end of a wood table and stood while I introduced him to Angella. He then motioned for us to join him at the table. Behind him hung several monitors, all off, except one that displayed various weather and sea condition numbers, all meaningless to me.

Clearly his demeanor toward me had changed. He wore the expression of a man with the weight of the world on his shoulders. "Jimmy, I owe you an apology from our last meeting. I had no idea you were with law enforcement. To say the least, our people were surprised when they found your weapon and shield. So, I hereby apologize, both for myself and for them. I trust they did not injure you."

I massaged my throat, which now only throbbed occasionally. "Accepted," I reluctantly answered. "Now we can move on."

"What's you role in all this? State Police working for SPI. What gives?"

"Rangers, not Police and not exactly working for SPI. I'd characterize what I'm doing is helping out—working with if you like—SPI. State often helps out in these situations. Two people died on the Island and SPI—Chief Duran—must clear them. Angella was assigned to work with me."

"What do you know of our operation?"

"Nothing official. Pieced together a lot of stuff, but nothing concrete."

"Just give me what you have."

"For starters, a Ranger was working undercover on the Gulf Mob or whatever their name is and was found dead on the beach at Padre. Another guy, going by the name of Heart, found dead of an overdose. He was tied to the drug trade, but I'm not positive how." I went on to tell him I thought a load of drugs was, or had been, delivered and that I believed terrorists were being delivered to the US in the next day or so. I told him about Mark's theory that a dam was involved, but did not mention Mark. I also told him that at least one terrorist, perhaps in the form of a Korean—North if I had to pick one or the other—was already in the country.

"For a guy who's picking around the edges you sure as hell did a good job."

"Thanks, that's how I earn my living."

"Okay, you leveled with me, I'll reciprocate. What I'm about to tell you is highly confidential. I received permission to speak to you and only you." He looked toward Angella and asked her to leave.

I cut that short. "Do what you have to do to get permission, but what I hear she hears."

He glared at me a moment, pushed back his chair as if to leave, then changed his mind. "If she can keep this to herself, I mean no reporting to Duran or anyone else, then I can go forward."

Boyle looked hard at Angella who thought for a long moment and then said, "I'll do what my partner does, nothing less and nothing more."

"If that means you will abide the information, I'll go forward."

Angella replied, "Whatever Jimmy does I do."

"Okay. Here it is. We have very reliable reason to believe North Korea is planning a major set of attacks on American soil. Speculation is that several dams are targeted. However, the dams may only be a diversion. The real target could be elsewhere. We don't know how many teams will be introduced into the country, but we know at least one team is coming through South Padre Island. Twenty men in all. Not all here mind you, but a total of twenty. I should say, twenty men plus—and here is where the problem is— nuclear, more accurately, atomic, weapons. The truth is, it doesn't much matter what the target is, just setting off a device of mass destruction in the USA will unleash mayhem."

I was struggling to grasp the magnitude of what he had just said. When I was growing up, folks had shelters, underground shelters, in case of a nuclear attack. But all that had gone by the boards and, to my knowledge, the country was totally unprepared for a nuclear attack. "My God!" was all I could think to say. "My God! So that's why the public hasn't been warned!"

"Exactly. Warn them to what avail? There'd be mass panic if we announced a possible nuclear blast anywhere in the country. What precautions do you take for a nuclear reaction? If we knew where and when, we could evacuate. But we can't evacuate every city, so either we stop them or we deal with the consequences."

"And they are what?"

"That's not my mission. My mission is to stop them before they get in the country, or at least render their nuclear capability useless."

"And what does that mean? I mean in real terms, how do you do that?"

"Atomic devices of the type we are concerned with have several fundamental pieces, all of which must come together at the right time. There is the fission material, and there is the package that holds the material. Of course there's the detonation portion. All we need do is capture the detonator and the rest is useless."

"I thought they were assembled as one device."

"That's how we do it. But, and here's where we catch a bit of a break, the North Korean's don't trust anybody, even their own. Give a guy one of those devices, and he could turn on them. So they give a device to one guy and the detonation trigger to another. The two don't know each other and they must meet up. My job is to prevent that meeting."

Still in a daze, I asked, "So what are we looking for?" I could never have figured this out on my own. Having never dealt with atomic bombs I had nothing to fall back on. I wouldn't know one if I was sitting on it.

I glanced in Angella's direction, and if I hadn't known her so well, I would never have seen the terror in her eyes. Her face, however, gave nothing away. I pitied anybody playing poker with her.

Captain Boyle continued his briefing. "Apparently, in the '50s and '60s we built and later destroyed several Special Atomic Demolition Munitions. You may have heard of them referred to as suitcase bombs. Well, we recently found out they weren't all destroyed. Several, all W54s, have now been traced to our pals in North Korea. The W54 is a cylinder 40 by 60 centimeters weighing 68 kilograms. That's about a hundred fifty pounds, case you're wondering. Actually, much less if they reduce or remove the shield.

"You telling us that these puppies are in transit to the US right now."

"Worse. One or more may already be in country."

I took a deep breath to clear my mind. "Are you at liberty to elaborate, or must we continue to guess?"

"I can't tell you everything, but that is where the missing video files are critical. When we went on red alert late last week, all patrol boats automatically began recording video at all times when their engines were on. With memory size and cost any more, it's trivial to store each day's missions. What that means is the patrol vessel Mark dispatched with the radioman was being video recorded. Mark has the video of that mission."

I was puzzled and skeptical. Mark was not known as one who toyed with the rules or even came close to their boundaries. If Boyle didn't have my undivided attention before this, he sure had it now.

Boyle continued, "We have to back up a moment and you'll see how this comes together. The radioman was a substitute; he's gone missing now and, when I tell you his real name, or at least one of his names, you'll understand our concern. Anyway, the man was a plant. The Gulf gang behind this, as you know, have been taxing our resources by coming into US waters and then calling for help. Usually they run when we dispatch. But as you recall, the one Mark dispatched when you were here reported back that there was no vessel at the distress location."

I did of course recall that, because Mark and I discussed the problem. I also remembered that Mark had dispatched the radioman because they were short on people.

"As luck would have it, we caught a break. Our satellite happened to be passing overhead at the time, and we have a sat picture clearly showing the so-called distressed vessel was indeed out there. The sat image clearly shows both vessels. So someone was lying."

"Luck or was it planned?" I am not a big believer in coincidences. Sure, we catch breaks all the time, but to have a satellite going overhead at the exact right time was a stretch.

"Command actually redirected the satellite because of the ongoing operation. We get pictures every four hours instead of once a day. But that of course is classified information."

"My lips are sealed," I replied, trying to communicate to Boyle that we were on the same team. I still wasn't sure he was buying it.

He continued in the same command tone he had taken since the beginning of the briefing. "Turns out it was the plant who lied. He was one of ours originally, but turned and was working for the drug cartel. Cutting to the chase, they smuggled a Korean and at least two other people right onto our dock using one of our own vessels."

Now I understood what had Mark worried. It had happened on his watch and, in the military, if it was on your watch you're guilty. Period. End of discussion. His career was indeed most likely over. "And that's what's on the video Mark has?"

"Exactly."

"So why did he go to so much trouble and risk his career to keep the video from you? That's not like him at all."

"Speculation at this point. But the video also captured your man Harreson Nelson on the target vessel alive and well. Also on board was a guy going by the name of James Alterez. His full name is James Alterez Santiago, brother of Mark's fiancé. Now you see why we're concerned? We need to investigate Mark's actions."

"Most definitely," I confessed. "Most definitely."

"Ok, so who's this mysterious radioman? And why the hell isn't he in the brig?"

"Name's also one you know. Jason Monroe Hardwick. His friends called him Heart."

TWENTY-NINE

"I suppose this is the point in the conversation where you demand the video," I said.

"One would think this is the point in the conversation where you break your ass to get it for me without my having to ask."

"One condition."

"Speaking of the brig, you're not in much of a position to be making demands. Does the word treason ring a bell?"

"There's no need for threats. I have no intention of breaking any laws, which, I most likely know a bit better than you anyway. Here's my condition. Chief Duran, Angella and I watch it with you. Since we already know the gross details, a few finer points won't be in violation of state secrets—and will serve to keep us all on the same page."

"Actually, we're going to do one better than that. Now that you've been briefed, I'm going to bridge you to the command center. As I said, we're just a tiny piece of a massive operation. Ours is different in that we've had two murders, but there's been several other landings. One in New Jersey, in a cove behind Sandy Hook, one in Oakland, and another on Puget Sound just above Seattle. General Jamison is in charge of the operation. I'm reporting directly to him for this mission."

"General Maxwell Jamison! Thought he retired years ago."

"He did. But the President called him back after nine one one. He handles operations when they go code red. Has jurisdiction over all the branches. You get respect when you have the President's direct line."

"I'll get the Chief on the line," Angella said. "Don't want to keep the General waiting."

I had heard stories about Jamison ever since my first days with the Rangers. He was a decorated officer in Vietnam, having served, if my memory's correct, with the Air Force Rangers. He led a brigade into a fierce battle during the Eastertide Offensive and was taken prisoner with three others and tortured for weeks in North Vietnam.

He escaped his captors, hid in the jungle overnight, and the next morning went back and released twenty others. He was awarded both a Purple Heart and a Congressional Medal of Honor.

Man is fearless. I know this because my boss, Lt. Contentus, was one of the men he freed. The man was a legend, well connected politically, and perhaps the most powerful person in the country in time of crisis.

Jamison being involved meant one thing and one thing only. The President of the United States was being briefed by the hour. No wonder everyone was walking on eggshells.

And it also meant that Contentus had lied to me, or should I say, didn't tell the full truth, when he said he was disobeying the Governor's orders because it was a Ranger who had died. Contentus was working with Jamison and I was being used as bait. There was no question in my mind, Contentus would lay down his life for the man who freed him from that hell hole in North Vietnam. Now he had volunteered mine.

Angella handed me the phone, saying the Chief was on the line.

Without preamble, I said into the receiver, "We're at the Coast Guard Station. Need you here as fast as you can get here. We need you to bring the videotape. It's in a watertight seal in the toilet bowl in the men's room outside your office. Please don't open it."

"Now we wait," I said to Boyle, "unless there's more you care to tell us. If we had known all this initially, we might have been able to nab a few of the terrorists, maybe even prevent the second death."

"You got your job to do, I got mine. I can't free-lance." He glared across the table at me, before he added, "In the military we follow orders."

"Okay, gentlemen," Angella broke in, "we've been making progress, let's leave the testosterone out of this. One thing is clear; the bad guys know how to work the seams. They're counting on a lack of cooperation—or at least communication—among all the agencies. INS had a guy planted in SPI, and we had no idea. I'm a low-life in the scheme of things, and even I know that's not the way to run the railroad."

"While we're waiting," I said, "Angella, can you get us a list of whatever they found in the raid? I'm looking for what the Korean had in his room. He sure didn't have much when he went on the beach. Had to have left something behind."

Angella placed a call and was back in less than two minutes with the answer. "Nothing but a broken flashlight," she announced.

"Oh shit!" exclaimed Boyle. "He's the detonator man."

"I don't understand," I said, looking to Angella to see if she had caught on. She looked just as confused as I was.

"Source of power. The broken flashlight means he was making the battery pack. That's the easy part. But he had to have the proper cord, or at least the plug that mates with the detonator. Can't very well walk into *Radio Shack* and ask for an A-bomb adapter!" He looked from one to the other of us and then said, "This confirms that our information on the security alert is accurate."

"But what about clothes? Surely, he had pants, a shirt, and I bet shoes."

Angella replied, "Not according to what they found. He had no pants, shirt or shoes when we chased him."

"Someone else in that house then was working with him," I said. "Man can't get far with nothing to wear."

Just then, one of the monitors came alive. The camera was focused on a dozen or so screens, some with outlines of the United States overlaid with flashing lights of various colors.

"That's the headquarters control room. Those green lights are surveillance planes, the blue are helicopters."

"What's that one?" I pointed to a red circle moving across an outline of North America.

"That's a recon satellite. And the white dots below it are what it is seeing."

"White dots don't tell you much."

"Each of those can be expanded and drilled down on. That's being done in another room. They can just about see who's on deck of a freighter if they want. Well, it's not actually that precise, but pretty close."

Boyle hit a switch, and another monitor in our room came to life.

"What's that?" I asked.

"That's our piece of the universe. See the coast line of South Padre Island?" He flashed a red dot on the screen and focused our attention on what I had thought to be simply a random line.

"Now I see it, yes. Are those green and blue lights planes and helicopters?"

"That's right?"

"Then you have it all covered. They can't get ashore."

"That's our plan, but those bastards are clever."

Chief Duran was ushered into the room. Captain Boyle stood and shook hands. The Chief handed a plastic container to Boyle without saying anything.

Angella nodded, but was lost in thought. I'd seen that look before and knew she was working her way through whatever it was that troubled her.

Boyle said, "I've sent word to the General that Chief Duran is here and that we have the video. He should be with us in a moment."

I thought of Mark and how a wonderful career had become messed up and, from what I could discern, it was the classic story of boy meets girl, boy does dumb stuff. I replayed our conversation with Trich and recalled that she had shown us pictures of her mother and brother, but not of her father. Where was he in all this? With all the money that must have gone into this plan, it was hard to believe the head of the local drug organization was not involved when his son was up to his eye lashes in it.

Suddenly Angella announced, "I got it! Remember when you stopped me from shooting him in the head?" Without waiting for a reply, she continued, "The reason you had time to stop me was because I hesitated. I was worried that I hesitated because I was afraid to pull the trigger. Now, I recall I hesitated because I was momentarily trying to figure out what was wrapped around his neck. At the time I thought it was an unusual necklace of some sort, a braided chain actually. But with the information we just received, I'm now convinced it was a braided cord—an electric cord."

"The missing adaptor!" I exclaimed, "So the Korean has it."

A booming voice filled the room. "Who is that woman and what is she doing there?" the voice demanded. "I authorized no woman! I assume the man on the right is the police chief and the other must be Redstone!"

"Yes, Sir," Captain Boyle replied, sitting up even straighter at the sound of the voice. The image on the monitor was now centered on a man with four stars displayed on each shoulder. "I authorized her, Sir. This is Officer Angella Martinez of the South Padre police force. She's working with Ranger Redstone."

"Should have told me before this! Surprises are not in the cards. Contentus told me about Redstone and he did mention he was working with someone. Okay, then. I trust Contentus to get it right. Redstone, you come highly recommended, so don't let us down."

"I'll try not to, Sir," I replied, stalling to get comfortable with the situation.

Boyle asked, "Sir, do you want briefed on where we are?"

"Not necessary. Been listening to your conversation for a few minutes, so I know what's going on down there. Let's have a look at the vessel tapes."

"Yes, Sir," Boyle answered. "This will take a moment. Got to dry the capsule and get it open."

Boyle walked across the room and opened a door, revealing a small control room with equipment lined along two walls. I followed him into the room and nodded to Angella to brief her boss, while we got the video going. I wanted to be sure Boyle used the video he had been handed. I didn't want any possible substitute going down.

Boyle retrieved a hair dryer and carefully dried the capsule. When the moisture was gone, he opened a small vial of liquid and placed a few drops along the sealed edge. In a few seconds the top slid off, allowing Boyle to slip the flash drive out.

While he was working, Boyle said, "These sealable containers work wonders for us. They seal within seconds with hand heat and lock moisture out. We use them for all manner of things on the vessels. Okay, got it, let's see what we have." He inserted the drive in a wall-mounted device, pushed a few buttons, grabbed a hand-held clicker and ushered me back to the main room.

Another of the blank monitors came alive and, immediately, the bow of the Coast Guard vessel appeared, slowly backing away from the dock. Boyle put the image on fast forward, and we could see the time elapse as the boat cut through the slight swell, just as I remembered it the day we were out there.

Twenty minutes on the display timer went by in less than a minute with nothing but blue water breaking over the bow. Then, suddenly, an image appeared dead ahead. Boyle adjusted the controls, the speed came back to normal and the sound of water washing against the boat filled the room.

"You getting the feed?" Boyle asked, looking up at the General's image.

"Coming across fine. Let's see what we have."

The voice of Seaman Smith, the radioman who was, in reality, the person we knew as Heart, could be heard speaking with the target vessel. He hadn't bothered with normal protocol, simply saying, "I'll be alongside in five minutes. Have the cargo ready."

Boyle whispered to me, "What you just heard is important for your friend Mark. I suspect this is what he wanted to protect. It's clear Smith was a plant. He knew all along he was going to pick up cargo. That's not Mark's fault. It's the service's fault for allowing a bad egg in. If these guys had jumped Smith, then Mark would be accountable because it happened on his watch. There will be an investigation, but so far, based on what we just heard, I'm on his side. Just so you know."

"Postmortems later," Chief Duran lectured, "let's see this to completion."

In a few minutes, the Coast Guard vessel pulled alongside what I guessed to be a forty-foot power-sports fishing boat equipped with fishing reels and seats for reeling in game fish.

The Korean, the same guy we chased onto the beach, appeared carrying only a small backpack and jumped onto the Coast Guard boat, Smith giving him a hand to steady him. Two other men followed and, without closer study, it was impossible to determine nationality.

"That it?" Seaman Smith asked.

"Get them to dock safely. That's all you need worry about," someone barked.

The boats then separated and Boyle hit the pause button. "Look at this," he said, flashing his red pointer at two people on the fishing boat. "Isn't that your guy Nelson?"

"And the other guy is Alterez! Alterez James Santiago to be exact. He's Mark's finance's brother and also the guy whose apartment the guy Heart, your Seaman, died in."

"Analyze this later!" the voice of General Jamison boomed. "Play it through."

The video restarted, and our guy Nelson could be seen using a cell phone, starting to work on a text, when Alterez came up behind him, a length of fishing line in his hand.

A second later, Nelson was lying dead in a pool of blood on the deck of the fishing boat. Alterez was signaling to the departing boat, motioning it to come back.

"What the shit's this?" Smith exclaimed when he came alongside.

"Never mind! Just get this guy on board!"

"Not a chance!" Smith replied. The boat started to move away and a shot rang out.

"Next one goes through your brain!" Alterez snapped. "Now get that fucking boat over here and do as you're told!"

When the dead man was loaded on the Coast Guard boat, Alterez jumped aboard. "Now get this tub back to dock as fast as you can," he said. "One peep out of you and I'll blow your brains out."

Again, there was twenty minutes of water swelling over the bow and again Boyle speeded up the video. Then the breakwater became visible and, soon, the swells disappeared, and the boat was moving in smooth water between the jetties. Something leaped in front of the bow and Boyle paused the image.

"What the hell was that?" Jamison demanded.

"Dolphins, Sir," Chief Doran said. "The boat is passing through their feeding area just off the park."

The video began again and people on *Fins to Feathers*, an eco-tour boat, waved as the Coast Guard vessel moved toward its dock. No one came out of the station to help, and Boyle said, "Notice no one is helping dock the vessel. That's because Mark—and you—are still out on the water. That was part of their plan. That allowed them to pull right up to our own dock and drop their passengers off. A lot of nerve, but well planned. They know our operation inside and out. Mark will have to explain how that came to be."

I let that remark go. "So now we know who killed Nelson. All we need now is to know who killed Heart."

"Focus on the big picture!" came the booming voice. "You got a terrorist running loose down there. Should have nailed him when you had a chance!"

By focusing on the small stuff, the everyday stuff, Angella and I had managed to gather a lot of valuable information that we would not now have if all we had done was concentrate on the *big picture*.

I wanted to say that to General Jamison, but again decided to hold my tongue. The man didn't seem amenable to accepting unsolicited comments.

"Okay, now, Gentlemen," Jamison said, "we need to stop them from smuggling the other terrorists into the country. The ones with the actual bombs. We've got to assume that the first ones from each team are already here. We've got to be ready for them in New Jersey, Oakland, and Washington. Boyle, you are responsible to see to it the second man doesn't get through. You're authorized to use whatever force you need to prevent it. I will turn over the Gulf air task force to you immediately. Stop those bastards at any cost!"

"Yes, Sir," Boyle replied, as the screen went blank.

Boyle turned to me. "You heard the man, Redstone, you're job down here is finished. This is a blockade operation now. You can go back to Austin, or wherever, and let us get on with stopping these terrorists before it's too late."

That was the last straw. The chair fell over when I stood to face him. I was aware that both Chief Duran and Angella were also on their feet. Captain Boyle had braced himself and was ready for me. I was fully aware that to strike an officer on government property was not the smartest thing a person could do. I simply didn't care.

"Stop this instant!" commanded Chief Duran. "Redstone, back away immediately. Boyle, you do likewise! I don't know what it is with you both, but whatever it is, get over it!" Duran waited to see what I would do.

To my credit and contrary to what my gut told me to do, I stepped backward. Boyle, on the other hand took a step forward.

"I wouldn't do that if I were you," Duran said to Boyle, his chin set hard. "I may not have jurisdiction on government property, but

I'll sure be a witness at your court-martial should you lay a hand on any of my officers. That clear enough for you?"

"Where do you come off threatening me on my own base?"

"You want it blunt, I'll give it to you blunt! If you and your operation hadn't screwed up, we wouldn't have two dead bodies laying about—and we sure as hell wouldn't have nukes running wild in our country! You want to lay this on Lieutenant Cruses, you just go right ahead. But I'll remind you that he worked under your command and it was your command that was compromised. Now we have a killer or killers running free, and it's my job to find them. I can't deal with the bigger picture—and from the looks of it, neither can you! So stand down and cooperate."

Boyle pointed to the door. "All of you get out of here. I've got work to do. There's another drop tonight and we need to be ready. Goodnight, Gentlemen."

The three of us walked out together. Duran said, "You don't know how tempted I was to let you have at that arrogant son of a bitch! If this was SPI, I would have allowed it go a few rounds. But hitting him here is a Federal offense, and the FBI has no sense of humor for this type of thing. He was baiting you. Listen, the drop is tonight. I think we all now know that by now. But what you don't know is why. I'll tell you why. A big sailboat race started yesterday and ends early in the morning off the breakwater. From Corpus to South Padre. The water will be full of sailboats and chase boats. One or two more or less, how will the Coast Guard sort them out?"

"Cancel the race," Angella exclaimed, her voice surprisingly strong, considering she was speaking to her boss.

"Went round and round on that. The question is what do they tell the racers? The press gets a hold of the story, and the next thing you know, the nuke issue will be page one. In short, they can't stop it, and with it, the terrorists have the edge."

"Stop it, anyway," Angella persisted. "Surely, national security comes above all else. What do they say when the bomb goes off? Oops!"

"Oops worked when the World Trade Center came down," Duran replied, a wry smile on his face. "Bush blamed the guy before him, the Commission was politically correct and blamed anyone who drew a breath. In the end, they paid off the victims, attacked Afghanistan and then they attacked Iraq, which had nothing to do with the attacks on 9/11, and life went on."

"So," I said, "I suppose when the bomb goes off, we'll blame some luckless guy in Homeland Security and attack North Korea."

"Maybe we'll attack Pakistan, who the hell knows. For all the hell we know, they might even attack France! Depends upon which country we're most pissed off with when the time comes."

"You guys are sure cynical," Angella replied. "I think they know exactly who to blame."

"That's never been the issue in Washington and never will be," I replied. "They're about politics, and politics will determine what happens when these guys break through the front lines."

"And our immediate job," Chief Duran injected, "is to see that the front line is not breached. So the two of you get back to work and flush the rats from their holes. We don't have much time left. And, may I remind you, you don't take orders from the Coast Guard."

THIRTY

"Okay, Mr. Redstone," Angella said when the Chief was gone. "You have to admit that had I plugged that Korean character, there wouldn't be a bomb threat, at least not from this neck of the woods."

"Hindsight is indeed wonderful. But you'd be on leave, wondering if you'd ever work again. You think the Government would come to your rescue and say thanks for keeping the nukes out?"

"What do we do now?" she asked, changing the subject.

"We need to find several people. Alterez is one. We can lock him up if we catch him. The Korean is another, but I doubt we can find him. He's gone to ground. Paco is here to lead the shore expedition, so he's fair game."

"Don't leave out Joy and her husband," Angella added. "That's a pretty good list," she concluded. "You know, we didn't hear back from the stakeout at Joy's. Let me check."

"Shit," she exclaimed a moment later. "You're not going to be happy! And neither is the Chief." She held up her cell phone so I could see the picture of one, James Alterez. "Leaving Joy's apartment about two hours ago. While we were in with Boyle."

"Did he drive away or walk?"

"Walked. Went a block and then ducked back onto the beach. We didn't leave follow orders, so they didn't follow. Chief's now got an all points watch out for him. Armed and dangerous. Follow, but don't apprehend without backup."

"We can't add anything there," I said, "so who do you suggest is next on our list?"

"How about Trich? Her brother is certainly the key player. The more we know about him, his friends, his habits, his hangouts, the closer we can get to him."

"Good idea." I dug out my cell and sent a text to Trich: **Are you available to talk? Angella and I would like to visit with you.**

Almost instantly, the reply came: **at home in Matamoras. You are welcome to visit. Let me know when. I will meet you at bridge. Just walk across. You will need passports.**

"The passports might be a problem. Let's see if Chief Duran can work his magic. After his go-round with the INS guy they may lock us up."

"Speak for yourself. I have a passport, so I'll have no problem."

"Let's stop for a quick bite to eat on our way over. Any place come to mind?"

"In Port Isabel there's a place to get a quick fish sandwich."

Walking into *Pirates Cove* restaurant, we came face to face with a pirate. Actually, a good-looking young lady pirate of high school age hard at work hand drawing Henna tattoos on people. "Hey," I joked, "how about drawing a bull's-eye on my forehead."

"Arr, Matey," she replied out of the side of a scrunched up mouth, her right eye closed in an exaggerated wink. "Get ye a pint o' grog. I be ready for ye then. Twenty shillings it be."

"On second thought, I'll pass," I called to her from the restaurant door. "Catch you later." There already seemed to be a bulls-eye on my butt, no sense confusing anyone.

"Landlubber," the young pirate exclaimed, turning to finish the gorgeous bird she was drawing on a woman's arm.

While we were waiting for our fish platters, I asked Angella the name of the restaurant.

"With the pirate out front, what else would you expect? It's called *Pirates Landing* and has been here a long while. Rumor has it that at one time actual pirates made their headquarters on this site."

"Not that much seems to have changed, judging from what's going on."

An hour later we were in Brownsville and Duran had our passage to Mexico arranged. We parked in the visitor lot and approached the bridge. INS was waiting and we continued across the border without incident.

Trich met us at the far side and we walked to her house. Worry lines showed on her face, and her lukewarm greeting was in stark contrast to her animated conversation at the airport while we waited for Nora to arrive.

The family compound was less than ten blocks away, surrounded by a brick wall and an iron-gate entrance. She pushed a button, said a few words in Spanish, and the gate slid open. It opened only wide enough for us to walk through and immediately began to close behind us. If you were in, you were in, and if you were out you remained out. And I silently added, *as befits a drug lord.*

The grounds were magnificently groomed, with flowering plants tastefully arranged around a large water monument. A clay tennis court was positioned off to the side of the house, and the corner of what I supposed to be a large swimming pool peeked out from the back of the main house on the other side. If you lived here you'd have no reason to leave.

As we walked, Angella filled Trich in on what we knew of Mark. It was obvious the two had not spoken for a while. Trich was excited to hear that Mark was recovering and anxious to get all the news, stopping several times to digest what Angella was saying.

Trich led us around the side of the main house, down a winding path, toward one of the several smaller living quarters located beyond the swimming pool. "This one is mine," she announced. "That one is my brother Alterez's, and that far one is for my other brother, Juan Roberto, when he moves home."

"Where is Juan Roberto now?"

"In school in China. Father thought it would be a good idea for the family to have ties to different parts of the world. He's in his last year at the university."

"And where is Alterez? If I recall, his name is Alterez James. Or is it James Alterez?"

"His given name is Alterez James Santiago. But when he's in the US, he goes by James Alterez. He says he fits in better that way."

She said that with no trace of concern, as though it was a given and nothing was wrong with changing one's name to fit the circumstances.

I asked, "And when your father goes to the US, what name does he use?"

Her eyes tightened before she answered. "I know nothing of what my father does or where he goes. He refuses to talk to me about such things, so I don't know."

"Is he here? I mean if I wanted to could I speak with him today?"

Trich's face grew even tighter, and she turned to face me directly. "Did you come to see me or to pry about my father?" she demanded. "If you came about my father, you can leave right this minute!"

"I was just asking. We came to talk to you, but I just wanted to know if he was here or not?"

"I have not seen my father in many months. Not since May." Tears formed in her eyes and she said, "My mother smiles and says everything is okay, but I know something's wrong. He often is gone for a few weeks or even a month or so, but never this long. Even Alterez is gone more than he usually is." She wiped her eyes. "I'm sorry, I'm very concerned. Pardon me."

"We understand," Angella said, "we're here to help."

"Help. In what way can you help?"

"Help find your brother—and your father."

"But you are police. Did they do something wrong?"

I didn't want Angella to have to decide what to say, so I interceded. "We have reason to believe he's involved in criminal activity. If you know where he is, please tell us."

"In criminal activity! You expect me to help you against my own family!"

"You want to do right, do you not? You're not involved, so, yes, if they are doing wrong things I expect you to help."

"I don't know where my brother is. He hasn't texted me in a long time."

"We'd like to speak with your father," Angella broke in. "We have no information on what he's been doing, but if he's working with your brother, then we need to talk to him also."

"They don't get along very well."

"What does that mean?"

"No more questions about my family. It is disloyal to speak about your family."

"We didn't mean anything disloyal," Angella said. "By the way, did you happen to find a picture of your father?" Angella's voice had softened, as if the question had been an after thought.

"I have no pictures of him. He forbade us to take pictures. He said his enemies would use then against him. I didn't understand what he was saying, but he would never allow a picture. This is the first cell phone I've ever had with a camera, and I just got it last month. If he knew, he would destroy it."

"What does he look like? Can you describe him?"

"He's not too tall, dark hair. Handsome man."

"About how tall?" Angella inquired.

"I'd say five seven, maybe five eight. Mark is taller; he's just under six feet." She looked at me, and said, "About your height."

"Describe him, please," Angella continued.

"Many think he's American because of his light skin and light hair. Has a full head of hair. A good-looking man, even if I say so myself."

"Mustache?'

"Never wore one. Says it makes him look like a criminal."

"Slender?"

"No, rather full-bodied. Not heavy. No big belly or anything, but solid."

"Listen, if you come across a picture please send it along."

"Any chance his picture was ever in the paper?" I asked.

"Not that I recall."

Then it came to me, and I felt foolish for not thinking of it sooner. The motor bureau or whereever you get a license in Mexico would have a picture. And so would his passport. I excused myself and sent a text to Duran asking for pictures from one or the other. I wanted one so Trich could verify it for us.

That was not to be. In a few minutes, the answer came back: **What took you so long to ask? He has no driver's license and no passport. We've been working that angle for years.**

I asked Trich about the driver's license, and she replied, "No need for one. He has a driver. In Mexico, even I have a driver. Father would never allow me to go driving alone. Even when I walk to the bridge, he has people watching me. He is so old fashioned." She paused a moment, then appeared to think of something. "But the interesting thing I just realized is he let us ride horses anywhere we wanted to go."

"Horses," Angella responded. "Do you keep horses? I love horses."

"Come," she said, "I'll show you the stables. We have twelve horses, and we all love to ride. Alterez is the best. He has a way with horses. As a boy, he about lived in the barn, always had manure on his boots."

We followed Trich down a path that I hadn't noticed earlier, leading us to a field that must have been several acres of grass. Two large structures stood to one side, and I could see several horses grazing in the area behind the barn.

Angella cooed over several of the horses and received an invitation to come back and go riding with Trich the next week.

"Next time you come," Trich admonished, a soft smile forming at the corner of her lips, "come earlier, so there is light enough to see."

No sign of her brother or her mother. Certainly no indication that her father was anywhere in the vicinity.

The women hugged when we left and promised to be in touch very soon.

THIRTY-ONE

Halfway across the International bridge, with the Rio Grande River, or, as it is known in Mexico, the Rio Bravo del Norte, beneath us, the bell in my mind rang! I grabbed my cell and sent a text to Duran: **run Alterez's picture past the owners of the horse stables on SPI. My guess, he worked there. Are any horses missing? Need a search warrant for the Malcolm apartment. Looking for cocaine, particularly, residue of what was found in Heart. Also for traces of manure from Alterez. If you can find a picture of Joy's husband that will be good.**

I said to Angella, "I'm betting he'll move the aliens from the Gulf to the Bay by horseback! It all fits! He can bypass the motor sensors and go around the beach all the way. Even if they look down from above, they'll see horses and not ATVs. By the time they figure it out, the target will be long gone."

"Are you thinking what I'm thinking?"

"And that is?"

"We'll saddle up and intercept them."

"You like to ride, here's your chance."

"Like the good ole' Wild West."

I checked my watch. "Chief said the race ends in the morning. That would put the boats off the north coast when? About three, maybe four in the morning?"

"Four or five even, hard to tell."

"That will give us time to get there." It would be close to midnight when we got back on the Island. There would be just enough time to get everything ready and go meet up with them.

By the time we got to the SPI bridge, we had our answer, but it was somewhat confusing. Yes, Alterez worked for Island Stables and yes two horses were missing.

The puzzling piece is why only two horses when we expected at least one person and a nuke. Angella supplied the answer when she said, "One for Alterez, one for the person he's smuggling in. Maybe the nuke is coming another way."

I briefed Duran on what we planned to do. He wanted to alert the Coast Guard and have them stationed in the bay.

"Not a good idea," I said into the phone. "Let's do this with people who really know the bay and the island. How about the wildlife deputies. They have boats and know how to chase people in the weeds. And besides, if our side has sensors, so does their side. That's how Paco evades you guys. He hears you coming. Angella and I will ride up the bay side of the island and get in position to intercept them. They wont even know we're there."

We went back and forth several times but, finally, Duran agreed, with the proviso that he coordinate the effort with all the other services.

I went to my room to pick up shoes suitable for riding and a hat to make me look like I knew what I was doing sitting on top of a horse. A baseball cap just didn't cut it. I changed into jeans and a long shirt.

A few minutes later, Angella and Duran came by to drive us to the stables. Duran had his camera, and said, I'm going out to the stables with you two. Wouldn't miss this photo op for the world. It's all cleared with the County. The stable folks will meet us out there. The Coast Guard is going along. They say they know every inch of the bay better than the wildlife folks. It's Boyle's operation. The man's tedious."

"How'd you pull that off?" I asked. "Can't imagine they'd even let me near the operation."

"Easy enough. I promised to include them in the credit if we catch the bad guys and, if something goes wrong, it's on you. Even your boss has approved, not that you'd ever think to include him in your plans."

"Just an oversight," I said. "Meaning to call him, slipped my mind." Even Duran had spotted the bulls-eye.

"Seems that's been happening to you consistently for a while, from what I hear."

"Work does have a way of consuming me."

"The search warrant was just approved. Good idea. I'll let you know what we find. Going over there after I drop you guys off to observe in person. Had to let the County in on that also. Just good relations and all."

The horses were ready when we arrived at the stables, and the Chief, true to his word, took several pictures of Angella and me riding off into the sunset along the bay. Except there was no sunset, just a waning moon high overhead.

"I'll take a five by seven of that last one," I called to Duran, wondering if it would end up on my desk or in an obit notice.

By my calculation, we had at least three hours, maybe even as much as six, before the excitement, if any, was to begin. Not to worry, Angella had brought backpacks, or more accurately, horse packs, with enough food and other supplies to allow us to stay out two days if necessary.

As I had already found out, even potty stops presented no problem for my partner. I admired her verve and intelligence. She had great instincts as to when to break into a conversation and when to remain silent. We seemed to play off each other naturally. She certainly had a natural curiosity if you will, for investigation and the stamina to follow through.

I wondered if she would consider applying for acceptance into the Rangers. I was sure she had been in law enforcement long enough, but I didn't recall the exact rules.

We trotted up the bay in silence, listening for sounds of life along this almost untouched part of the Island. Off to our right, across a wide, grassy, and perhaps swampy, expanse of land rose sand dunes built of sand blown there from the Gulf beach. The farther we traveled, the more barren and breathtaking the terrain became. Here and there were scattered trailers, some abandoned, some where people had set up housekeeping. Who could blame them? Less than five miles to town and you could live as though you were on the moon.

A few night-working egrets stretched their necks and continued foraging as we rode silently past. The horses were accustomed to this area and moved sure-footed, even when the sand gave way to water or grass.

I hadn't been on a horse for over a year, and I knew I'd be sore when this was over, but just how sore I had no way to anticipate.

Angella seemingly took to her horse as though she had been born in the saddle. Every now and again, I saw a glimpse of her face, usually in profile, and it seemed that serenity had settled on her, removing all traces of the harsh lines she often displayed. She was absorbed in her own universe where all was right with the world.

Most certainly, this journey north along the west coast of South Padre Island bore no resemblance to the world that waited for us within hours, a world where one rogue atomic bomb could wreak havoc for all Americans forever.

What would the US response be to an atomic weapon detonating on its soil? Would North Korea cease to exist? If so, how? What would China say about that? They shared a land mass, and how would the US control the fallout, both radioactive and political? That was all way above my pay grade. Was even the President prepared to deal with such a contingency? All I knew was that it was my duty to try and stop the nukes from being introduced in the first place. Unlike what Captain Boyle might have thought, I did have the big picture in mind. Only thing is, I only know how to execute one small piece at a time. Enough small pieces done well and the whole *is* solved—or so I wanted to believe.

In some endeavors, the consequences of failure are so great that to dwell on them freezes action. You must focus entirely on the positive, concentrating on what your opponent could do and what he's most likely to do. This was one of those situations where failure was not an acceptable option.

After nearly two hours of steady movement north, Angella held up her hand. I pulled alongside, thinking she wanted to take care of nature. Instead, she pointed to a deep cove cut into the marsh a quarter mile ahead.

I followed her hand movements and finally saw what she was gesturing at. A fishing boat was tucked into the cove. At first I thought it was abandoned, washed up by last year's hurricane Dolly. But Angella put her finger to her lips and then pointed again.

I couldn't see what it was that she was so concerned with.

She leaned close and softly said, "Most fishing boats out here are shallow. This one seems to have a small cabin. That's what first caught my eye. Then I saw a glint of something moving. Can't see anything now. There may have been the silhouette of a horse moving away from the boat. But I can't be certain of that, or what it was—if anything."

"We're sitting targets out here," I said, stating the obvious. "We have to get down and scout on foot."

"What do we do with the horses?"

"Not much we can do. Tie them to the brush and hope they're not seen."

We slipped off the horses and walked them a bit inland. The terrain was essentially flat and devoid of trees. No place to hide. I hadn't thought about how exposed we would be, always assuming Alterez, or whomever we were trying to intercept, would be on the other side of the island picking up the merchandise.

When the horses were as secure as we could make them, I motioned to Angella to get down low. "Okay, best we can do. Let's move in and see what's up. I'll circle around and come from the north. When you see me approach, you come from the south. If you shoot, be certain you know where I am."

"Same goes for you," Angella smiled. "Be careful, this ground tends to be swampy. It's mostly hard-packed sand, but you can dig in if you need to."

"Thanks. Just stay low." I started off to circle the boat, keeping as low as my knees would allow. This certainly was not an assignment for a guy my age. Before I left, I instructed Angella to text in our situation. I told her to provide the location of the boat, but to tell them to stay far away. Didn't want the bad guys spooked.

It was slow going and several times my feet hit watery sand. I felt and saw small animals skittering away all around me. I had no idea if alligators inhabited the marsh, but I knew of no reason why they wouldn't. It was warm and salty, a potent combination for all types of reptiles.

Twenty minutes later, I had circled far enough around so that I was ready to move toward the boat from the north.

Angella, obviously following my movements, started forward when I did. "Shit," I thought, "If she can follow me, so can they."

As if on cue, a gunshot broke the silence. I fell flat, sand filling my mouth and nose in the process. I lay as still as I could while digging the gritty substance from my breathing passages. My molars were grinding against the sand residue and I used my tongue to clean them as best I could. Sand filled my throat, and I struggled to suppress coughing.

A second gunshot rang out. I buried my body even deeper. I couldn't determine the direction the gun was being fired. Toward me or toward Angella.

When I finally ventured to put my head up, Angella was nowhere to be seen.

I waited and still nothing moved.

I started forward, moving on my elbows and knees. My left shoulder would not support my weight and kept collapsing. At any moment, I expected another shot but, instead, I was greeted with silence.

Something was moving in the direction of Angella and I froze, trying to discern what it was. I could barely make out a large shadow thrashing toward Angella, but it was too dark to see what it was. I brought my gun into position to shoot, but had no clear target.

Then I saw movement on the far side of the boat. It appeared to be the back of a man's head facing toward where I had last seen Angella.

I aimed the Berretta is his direction, but the angle was wrong. I'd have to be standing in order to even have a chance at hitting him.

I started forward, still crouched low, fighting to get as close as possible before exposing my full body to the shooter.

I was finally in position to stand and, just as I did, a bird flew out of the tall grass directly in front of me. The noise the bird made lifting off was enough to attract the shooter's attention.

Startled, he turned in my direction, his pistol leveled at my head from over the bow railing. I was off balance and not able to bring the Berretta into position. I dove to the ground. I heard the bullet from his gun pass through the weeds just beside my head.

If I stayed here, it would be like him shooting fish in a tub. He had ducked down, so I fought to my feet, slipping in the soft sand. I charged the boat, praying that I arrived before he spotted me.

His head reappeared and I had no option but to continue forward. I was clearly visible, but for some reason his head again ducked behind the gunwale. Maybe he had slipped on something, but I wasn't waiting around to find out.

I charged, hoping to make it over the side and into the boat before he could get me lined up again. But, as Angella had pointed out, this boat was higher than a normal fishing boat and the railing was almost six feet above the marsh.

I was half into the boat when he reappeared, the gun raised in my direction. I was closer to him than he thought, and his angle was poor. I held onto the boat with my right hand and with my now barely functioning left, reached out to swat at the gun.

The momentum of the sideward movement caused my right hand to slip free of the boat.

Some days, luck works better than skill. This was one of those days. As I fell backward toward the sand, the extended fingers of my left hand grazed the barrel of his gun. That slight touch was enough to deflect it so that his next shot again missed.

He fell backward with the shot and, when my feet hit the ground, I bounded back upward with enough force to get my stomach over the top edge of the boat railing. Momentum carried me into the boat.

The gunman was lying about two feet from me, and I lunged for the pistol, which flew from his hand and landed about five feet away. He dove after it, and I landed on his back at the same instant he reached the gun. He tried to turn and point it at me. Again it went off harmlessly.

I was able to grasp the barrel and twist it back and to the side. The gun again flew out of his hand. As it turned out, I was surprised to find he could even pull the trigger these last few times because a bullet Angella must have fired had ripped through the muscle of his right arm, rendering it essentially useless. That had been why he could not keep his balance. He had slipped in his own blood.

His gun fighting days were over—even assuming he lived long enough to be taken out of here alive.

I called for Angella and received no response. I turned him over and discovered this was our missing Korean. No sense talking to him, I doubted he would understand what I was saying. I motioned to the front of the boat and he crawled in that direction on one arm, refusing to utter a sound. I wrapped a boat rope around him and tied him to a cleat.

Then I jumped over the side and ran to where I thought Angella was. She wasn't there. I called to her several times with no answer.

I searched frantically but didn't see her. The good news was that I found no blood.

The bad news was that I found no Angella.

After searching for several minutes to no avail I ran back to the boat and found our captive wrapping his useless arm with a filthy piece of shirt he had managed to rip off. He was still tied to the boat, but had worked the rope loose enough to move his left arm.

I searched him, found a knife that I confiscated and put it under my belt. I was about to go look for Angella when another shot filled the silence.

I fell to the deck and watched as a flock of ducks took to the air, flying directly over the boat on their way to safety.

Another shot sent another flock flying.

I crawled to the corner of the boat and peeked over the transom. My plan was to slip off the back and hide in the water.

I ventured another look, just before I launched myself over the side.

Someone was creeping toward the boat through the tall weeds at water's edge. I could just barely make out the outline of a person. I waited, trying to line up a shot.

The ducks were stirring up the marsh around the boat, as they began to land. With all the random motion, I lost track of the human figure I had been following.

I wanted to call out to Angella but thought better of it. Didn't want them to know how many we had. I kept my head down, waiting to see if I could see any movement.

The text buzzer went off in my jeans and I thought what a stupid time for the Chief to be calling.

Reluctantly, I slipped the cell out, and read the message: **Martinez: 2:50PM Where are you?**

I replied: **On the boat. Korean tied up. Alone. Where are you?**

Martinez: 2:51PM Just south of the boat near the stern.

I answered. **Slip over to the boat from the stern. I'll cover you.**

Within ten seconds Angella appeared at the transom, and I pulled her aboard. We both lay quiet, our heads below the gunnels, listening for sounds of others.

Nothing.

I whispered, "Did you fire those last two shots?"

Her face set hard and she reluctantly answered, "Had to." Angella's peacefulness had vanished, replaced by anguish—and anger.

"That creep is our missing North Korean, just so you know."

"Should have shot him the first time! Woulda saved two perfectly good horses."

"You shot the horses!"

"He did, but didn't kill them. I put them down. Never want to do that again."

"Sorry." This loss was painful, but in perspective, not as painful as if it had been Angella. "Text this in. Have them come by boat for him. No helicopters. Don't want to tip them off."

She started to text the message and I put my hand over the screen. "No, come to think of it, without horses we can't track them. So, we'll stay here and let the bad guys come to us. Tell Duran where we are, but ask him to stand down."

"What about him?"

"We'll gag him and put him below. If he dies, I'll invoke the Big Picture rule taught to us by the good Captain. Bet I find the detonator cable down there."

I took the Korean below, tied him to a cot. Tied the rest of his shirt around his mouth and waved my pistol, as if saying I'd shoot him if he made any noise. I then ripped the place apart looking for the cord.

Nothing.

It was while I was searching the boat that things began to make sense, at least as far as my universe went. There were two-person teams. I had half a team in front of me. This half had the detonator adaptor. That meant the other half had the bomb.

We had been told that the reason the teams were not together was that the North Korean leadership was so paranoid they worried about the team using the weapon against them, or simply selling it to the highest bidder. Each team required both the bomb and the detonator adaptor specially fitted to the bomb. If that were the case then, the detonator would be similar to a unique key, maybe even pre-timed for a particular time—or pressure.

But in reality, you didn't need two team members to carry out the detonation. All you needed was the bomb and a detonator keyed especially for the bomb. Thus, one-person teams would work, provided the bomb was kept from the detonator until the last possible time. Following that logic, then the bomb would arrive under separate cover.

But then, why did Alterez have only two horses? A helper?

Shit! I motioned for Angella to come close. When she did, I said, "When we first got here, you said you thought you saw a horse."

"Yes I did. So? It could have been Alterez going to meet the drop."

"So, if you did, he's still out there. Alterez would have been on the other side of the island by now. It's not him you saw. But whoever it is didn't get involved in the shootout with us, so he may not be close, but he's there. That means Alterez, or whomever, is coming alone."

"Alone. I thought he was bringing the other team member with the bomb."

"The bomb maybe, but I'm convinced there's no second person."

The team members—or single member—was already here, having been driven ashore in the Coast Guard's own boat. I could only imagine how that would play in the press. No wonder Boyle was surly. I wouldn't want to face General Jamison with that bit of news.

What they were about to find out was going to make them even more surly, right to the very top. They had geared a mission to prevent the landing of terrorists by employing air, land, and sea forces. But it wasn't people they were looking for; it was merchandise. That's why they were using Paco. He was an expert in bringing merchandize across the beach.

When the bomb goes off, it hardly matters what the target was. The effectiveness of the United States military would forever be called into doubt. Trust would erode, both inside the country and with our allies all around the world. We were about to see the beginning of a downward spiral of our society, as government regulations increased to the point where the freedoms we cherish become textbook topics for our grandchildren to study.

North Korea, a country barely able to feed its own people, with almost no exports and little acceptance anywhere in the civilized world, would, with the detonation of even one atomic bomb within the borders of the United States, have done more permanent damage to the United States than all the might of the rest of the world combined.

If the military brass thought they had problems now, they were mere annoyances compared to what their lives were going be like when the public comes to understand that the mission to intercept these terrorists failed.

I texted my supposition to Duran, telling him to alert the CG to intercepting packages, and not just people.

Angella had returned to the bow and lay crouched, concentrating her vision north. As we had found out, keeping horses out of sight where there were no trees and mostly flat terrain was not easy. That meant Alterez would dismount up the beach and approach on foot.

Angella's cell phone began to vibrate, and she held it close to her lips and whispered, "Yes." She listened intently for over a minute and then said, "Got it, Bye."

She crawled to where I was positioned. "Seems you nailed it. Only it's the worst possible situation. The sailboat race got here faster than planned and, about two hours ago, several fishing boats began moving in close to the racers, looking as though they were going to run through the sailing fleet. Some, I understand, did. The fishing boats sent small fast boats toward shore with men laying low in them, some covered by tarps. This was all picked up by the surveillance planes and confirmed by under water sensors.

"Coast Guard cutters and several helicopters moved in. They dropped Navy Seals from the helicopters and from the decoy fishing ships you had observed. Spotter planes videoed the whole operation. The operation went flawlessly. They captured every alien and nothing came ashore."

"How do they know nothing came ashore?" I asked, wondering if I really had figured this out right.

"The operation called for a beach landing, if necessary, to round up anybody that managed to get to shore. The only boat moving out there was one kayak off the beach, it was a two-person kayak with only one person in it, and it turned back right after the action started without picking up anybody. There was no need to intercept him."

"They blew it!" I exclaimed. "That one person was Paco! I'll bet my shield on it. This operation was well planned. He went out with a two-person kayak to make them think he was going to pick someone up. That was a decoy. He was picking up the package. It was sent to him with underwater propulsion and a homing device. The Coast

Guard couldn't pick it out with all the turbulence from the boats and helicopters and Seals churning up the water. Beautiful! We created a screen for Paco! That was why the bad guys tipped this off ahead of time. They knew we'd overreact and throw everything we had at it. The bastards used our own operation to create the cover they needed! Got to hand it to them."

"Who's side you on here?" Angella asked, her eyes rolling in mock astonishment.

"Got to give credit where credit's due. A single man in a kayak. A single man riding horseback along the beach. What kind of danger does that present? It actually says a lot for our country where we allow, even encourage, people to do their own thing. In North Korea, they'd have shot Paco just for being where he wasn't expected."

"I trust you're not advocating that type of behavior."

"Just saying. You and I put our lives on the line every day to protect those freedoms. I wouldn't have it any other way."

"Just checking. So who are the people in the boats they captured?"

"My money says they were just a poor hapless bunch of Mexicans who paid hard-earned pesos to be smuggled into the United States. They had no way of knowing they were being used as props in a reverse sting operation."

"Poor souls. The further down the food chain you are, the harder life treats you. Do they ever catch a break?"

"At least for them it's better than being abandoned in the back of a trailer for three days in the scorching South Texas sun. Yes, maybe they did catch a break—only they'll never know it."

We sat in silence, our shoulders touching, both of us intently studying the far horizon thinking our own private thoughts.

Angella eventually asked, "So what're your plans after this? I mean you planning to get reinstated to the Rangers or what?"

"Before this all started, that was my plan. That's why I came down here, to rehab the shoulder, try to pass the physical." I nodded toward my hanging arm. "This is not working. Rehab might get it a bit better, but never enough to pass the Ranger physical. That's a long shot."

"You like being a Texas Ranger don't you?"

"I suppose I define myself that way. That's who I am." I studied her in profile, again aware of her sensual beauty, an undefined quality that I found particularly compelling. "Why do you ask?"

"Just asking is all."

"You thinking of joining?"

"Thought crossed my mind. I've not been in law enforcement long enough, but it's a nice dream, a nice goal if you will."

"Time will fix that."

"Need sixty hours of college. I dropped out after one year."

"So go back. You're good at this. A natural."

"If you can't get back on, what will you do?"

"Retire."

"I don't believe that for a minute."

"So what would you have me do, if I don't make it back? Can't exactly start my own Ranger outfit."

She went silent for a long while, and I assumed she had dropped the subject. Then she said, "How about coming down our way. You'd be perfect working with us."

"And doing what, exactly?"

"Chief of police for one."

"You got a chief, what else?"

"He'll move on soon. There're rumors floating about. You'd be perfect."

"To what end?"

"Then we can spend time together."

"Can't work on the same force if we spend time." I had to admit the spending time part sounded more than good. Wonderful, in fact.

"I'll work across the bay or with the County. We'll figure out something."

"I hadn't given any thought to ever doing anything outside the Rangers."

"Always time to think new thoughts. Aren't you the guy likes to pride himself about thinking out of the box?"

The prospect of working with Angella, actually of spending time with her not working, was exciting. This woman energized me as no other woman had ever done. I could see us together for a long, long time.

But this was neither the time nor the place for such thoughts. I said to her, "The sky's getting light. He'll be here soon. Unless you have a better plan, here's what I propose. I'll go out into the grass and wait out there. There's high grass over there that'll give me cover. You stay low in the boat. Find a porthole or a hole or something so you can see out, maybe even be in a position to take a shot if need be without showing your weapon. You see him, let him get in close, don't want him getting away out here."

I prepared to leave and she laid her hand on my arm ever so slightly and said, "Please be careful. When we separated before that was difficult for me, in more ways than one."

"I'll take care," I replied, excited about the prospects with her. I jumped off the boat and made my way to the only deep grass within sight. I stuck grass clippings in my hatband to disguise its shape.

Angella tucked herself away so I couldn't see her. I turned my cell off and remembered that I had forgotten to tell her to turn hers off. It was this type of rookie mistake that costs dearly.

I settled in to wait. The sand flies settled into a great breakfast of Texas Ranger ankle *à la carte*.

THIRTY-TWO

I had buried myself in high grass and built a mound of sand to steady myself while I studied the land as far as I could see. Nothing was moving out there. Water vapor lifting from the bay spread a shadowy haze over the scrub and made it difficult to pick out any distinctive shape. I reached for the binoculars and slowly scanned the north horizon, moving the glasses from left to right, keeping my elbows in the sand for clarity.

Nothing.

I worked my way back to the left, being careful to dwell in each zone to allow the shadows from the moisture to settle.

Still nothing.

Again, from right to left, this time a little farther into the horizon.

A muted spark of light caught my eye and I focused the binoculars on the spot.

Nothing.

Then the haze momentarily cleared, and a glint of light poked through, then it was gone.

I continued focusing on the spot, my eyes burning from the intensity. I wiped moisture from my eyes and refocused on the spot.

The haze was playing tricks because now nothing was visible.

Then suddenly, for the briefest of instants, I saw what could be a horse.

Then it was gone.

I continued focusing on the spot, and again the shape of a horse appeared as a pattern in the haze. Could this be a mirage? Wishful thinking? A random Rorschach pattern of fog allowing my mind to create it own image?

Doubt.

Several minutes passed, and the sun began to burn away just enough of the water vapor and with it the random shapes. Now I could clearly make out a horse, much too far away to hear its hoof falls.

As the distance shortened, I could make out a rider moving cautiously, but steadily toward the boat. He was leading a second horse. I trained my gun on the rider, but he was still too far away for a good shot.

I waited, prepared to spring into action the instant Angella made a move. I didn't know exactly where she was, so I didn't know her sightlines.

The rider was now bent low over the horse, his body mostly shielded from sight. It would take a perfect shot to bring him down, so I waited. He was moving slowly down the marsh, mostly in hard packed sand, but every now and then I could see water splash. The second horse was slightly off to the left, toward the bay, but moving steady, a load strapped to its back.

They were just about into my comfortable range, when he suddenly slid to the ground. I was sure this was Alterez, and I studied him as he unfastened the load from the trailing horse and let it fall to the ground. Turning, he slowly moved toward the boat.

With him off the horse, I lost my angle. He was no longer a good target from my position. I had to wait until he was about twenty yards from the boat, midway between me and Angella.

I stiffened in preparation for taking him out.

Angella should have challenged him by now, telling him to halt, put up his hands. Or shoot him outright. But, so far, silence.

I leveled my gun at his chest, my finger tight against the trigger. This was Trich's brother, and I felt sorry for her. But this was also the man I had watched calmly pull a wire through the neck of a Texas Ranger. Anyone who could do that is not human as far as I'm concerned. All personal feelings evaporated.

It was business now, all business.

A slight bit more pressure on the trigger and his life would end, just as Nelson's had, without warning. But Texas Rangers never shoot without warning. He had to be given a chance to surrender. It was our code, our bible if you will. I was not so far gone that I wanted to dishonor our tradition.

I sucked in a breath of air and pulled my knees under me preparing to stand. Dead or alive was okay by me, but not without warning.

The warning never came.

A strong hand clamped over my left shoulder, sending blinding pain to my brain. At the same time, a well-honed knife blade pressed against my throat.

"Drop the gun!" the voice behind me whispered, "or I'll cut your throat."

My gun fell to the ground.

"Now, stand and make no sudden moves." I knew the voice, but it took me a few seconds to put a face to it.

When I stood, he stood, and I felt the sticky warmth of my blood snaking down my neck. Any thought I had of breaking free evaporated, when I realized the blade was already deep into my skin. If I made the slightest movement, my carotid would be opened. Survival would be impossible.

The motion of me standing caught Alterez's attention, and he rushed toward me. He patted me down, found the Korean's knife and threw it on the ground. "What the hell you doing out here?" He barked, "You alone?"

Alterez was either acting or had no idea I was a cop.

"Answer me, you son of a bitch. What the hell you doing out here?"

I mumbled something, being careful not to cause my throat to move for fear of the knife going even deeper.

"Padre, loosen up so he can talk."

The knife moved away ever so slightly, but I had no illusions I could escape alive. Padre, Spanish for father! The puzzle pieces came together and locked solid. However, living long enough to hang this one on my wall was doubtful.

"Alone," I answered, "camping."

The blade tightened.

"Bullshit! You're lying! That's not your knife! You've been on the boat! What the hell's going on?"

I tried to say something, but the blade cut deeper.

"He's a cop!" The man behind me, the one called Padre, said. "Works with a girl! She's on the boat. I slipped off when they came up the beach."

Alterez fell to the ground and slowly crawled to the boat. When no shots were fired at him, he pulled himself up and disappeared inside. The man was surprisingly agile.

I was helpless to warn Angella or to do anything to stop him.

He called out. "The Korean's tied up. Shot in the arm."

"Oh, shit!" Alterez shouted, his voice muffled by the boat hull. "Slipped in this shit! Blood everywhere! There's no one else here!"

He came back on deck and called out, "Padre, we want our money, we better get the Korean across the bay, alive, with the cargo! The bleeding's stopped, but he's not in good shape."

My captor yelled back, "Get the boat started, I'll finish this one."

I felt the muscles in his arm tighten as he prepared to pull the blade across my throat. I held my breath, preparing one last lunge. I knew it was futile, but I refused to die without a fight.

I jerked my left arm back, intending to plant my elbow in his kidney.

As I moved, the knife sliced across my throat.

A shot rang out, and his grip loosened just enough so the blade did not cut deep enough to completely sever an artery, but blood was freely flowing.

I kicked backward with my right foot and pivoted to my left. The shot had caught Padre in the right shoulder, and when I hit his arm the knife flew off to the side. I bent to retrieve my gun, and the loss of blood caught up to me. I became light-headed. The ground swirled and I fell to my knees, helpless to pursue, and helpless even to crawl away from the line of fire.

I didn't know where Padre was and I assumed he had made it to the boat.

I grabbed my neck in a vain attempt to staunch the heavy flow, but the blood was spurting through my fingers.

I forced my eyes open and saw Alterez standing in the boat, his gun raised in my direction. He took careful aim, his arm now pointing straight at my head.

I was helpless to move, but even if I could have, it would have done very little good. My blood was pumping into the sand and even without his bullet I'd be dead in a matter of minutes. As it was, my heart was racing faster than I had ever felt it beat, and my vision was almost non-existent. Soon it would be over and my regret was that I had let Angella down.

Suddenly, with what little sight I had remaining, I saw Alterez's gun leap from his hand. I could only think Angella had something to do with that.

I heard the engine of the boat cranking, but it wouldn't catch.

Someone bent over me and I tried to roll away. Then, as if in a far away dream, I imagined Angella's voice telling me to let go of my neck. Then I felt her fingers gingerly peeling mine away. I was aware of warm blood pouring out, but I could see nothing.

"That looks nasty," I heard the woman in the dream say. "I don't believe he got the carotid, but we do need to stop this bleeding." Using Padre's knife, she cut a swatch out of my shirt, folded it, and pressed it against the wound. "Here, keep as much pressure on this as you can." She forced my hand back onto the wound. "We got to get you out of here."

I again forced my eyes to open and the vision of Angella cleared. With what little energy I could muster, I said, "Don't waste time on me. Stop them."

"Hey, she said, a slight smile at the corner of her lips, "for a class A detective you worry too much about the big picture. You should be sweating the small stuff."

"What are you saying?"

She reached in her pocket and produced a spark plug. "Don't know many engines that run without this."

She turned her radio on and when the signal came in, said, "Chief, you looking for the Santiago family, you got them. Son as well as the father. There's a wounded Korean on board in need of medical attention. Oh, Redstone managed to get his neck cut again. Yea, he's alive, but needs medical attention pretty quick."

The radio clicked alive. "Good work both of you. Seals are overhead and will be there in less than a minute. Look up, I bet you'll see their chutes. Got them on low level radar, they're hauling ass. Medivac right behind them. Keep that crazy Ranger alive two minutes. Whole friggin' hospital's on the way."

"Roger that. Bleeding's slowed. He's pale, but holding." Then she corrected herself. "He just passed out."

"Stay the hell away from the cargo!" the radio barked. "The idiots removed the lead casing to lighten it and the bloody thing is about as radioactive as it gets. They have Alterez on their screens. He's glowing like charcoal ready for a steak."

In fact, I hadn't passed out. I was working. The man with the knife I knew from the voice to be Joy Malcolm's husband. I had no doubt about that. He was also Alterez and Trich's father. Unfortunately, she will now have more pictures of him than she can bear to see.

Angella was sitting in the blood soaked sand, pressing the cloth against my throat. I said, "Ask the Chief what's happening in the other operations?"

When Angella didn't respond, I continued, "I mean in New Jersey, Washington, the other places?"

Angella had apparently keyed the mike, because I heard Duran's voice respond, "Hey, Ranger. You're job is done. Stop worrying about the rest of us and take care of yourself."

Before I could answer, the sky filled with kites. Angella bent and kissed my forehead. "Seals have landed. Behave yourself."

"What about the nukes?" I managed to ask.

"Duran says he doesn't rightly know." Angella answered. "I heard a few minutes ago they were tracking the radiation. Seems like, even with the shield in place, the stuff is radioactive. Communications with Washington is uni-directional. Defies gravity. Flows uphill. I guess we'll all know when we hear the big oops!"

"I love you," I said.

"Nice to know," the deep voice of a Navy Seal responded. "That's what they all say. Now. relax and go off duty. You did a good job. Now it's our turn."

With that, he shot something into my arm. All I remember after that was someone kissing my cheek.

I trust it was Angella and not the medic.

APPRECIATION

I write for fun. It can't be much fun for my wonderful wife, Mary, to know that I am spending vast amounts of time thinking about people she does not yet know, and may, in fact, never wish to have visit in our home. She is without doubt the most perfect life-partner a person could ever have.

This is not the first book I have written, nor, G-d willing, the last. However, it is the first book of mine to be published. I would like to take this opportunity to publicly thank those who have painstaking slogged through my several manuscripts and who have provided valuable feedback—and most importantly, words of encouragement.

The list is longer than I can account for here. In addition to my wife, my long-time friend, Burt Lazarow, deserves special mention. His advice and counsel have been invaluable. Fran Nichol, whose friendship I have cherished since high school, is also at the top of the list of those who are unwavering in their encouragement. Thanks also to Debi T. for her help with the manuscript.

David Harry can be reached at davidharry@hotray.com

For information about upcoming books and other items of interest please go to hotray.com.

Made in the USA
Charleston, SC
03 December 2010